FATHERS' DAUGHTERS

FATHERS' DAUGHTERS

Transforming the
Father-Daughter Relationship

(Formerly entitled *The Hero's Daughter*)

Maureen Murdock

FAWCETT COLUMBINE • NEW YORK

A Fawcett Columbine Book
Published by Ballantine Books

Library of Congress Catalog Card Number: 95-90672

ISBN: 0-449-91024-5

Cover design by Barbara Leff
Cover photograph by George Kerrigan

Manufactured in the United States of America

First Trade Paperback Edition: January 1996

10 9 8 7 6 5 4 3 2

For my father

CONTENTS

ACKNOWLEDGMENTS

A book is never the work of one person; this book had a cast of thousands. *Fathers' Daughters* tells the story of women I have worked with in therapy, UCLA writing classes, workshops throughout the country, and weekly women's groups dealing with the father-daughter relationship. Without their stories we would have no female perspective on what it is to be a father's daughter. Celeste Torrens brought her unique perspective and warmth to the father-daughter group she co-led with me. My agent, Beth Vesel, a father's daughter herself, encouraged me each step of the way to flesh out the paradoxes inherent in being a father's daughter. She guided *Fathers' Daughters* into the capable hands of Jöelle Delbourgo at Ballantine Books, who has been a wise and constant advocate. My editor at Ballantine, Joanne Wyckoff, challenged me to understand the difference between being a father's daughter and being a mother's daughter. My rewrite editor, Margaret Ryan, brought her laser-sharp perception and generous humor to unearth the book within the book. My dear friend Nora Dvosin, a writer, met with me for two years' worth of Tuesday nights so we could share meals and exchange ideas about each other's writing. I got the lion's share of our mutual editorial and culinary expertise. Along with Nora, the other women in our writers' group gave me valuable feedback and shared their experiences: Ann Glover, Susan King, Michelle Kort, and Aleida Rodriquez. Thanks to the women in my visioning group—Celeste Torrens, Bonnie Ban, Suzi Rudnick, and Terry Binkovitz—who supported my process and reminded me about the light at the end of the tunnel. The men and women in the couples' group in which my husband and I participate shared valuable insights about fathering and about their experiences of having been fathered: Marti Glenn, Ken Bruer, Greg and Judy Bravard, Janey Johnson, and Gary Bostwick. Valerie and Joe Bechtol and Meibao Nee provided me with nurturing writing environments in New Mexico when I began this book. Ironically, I wrote the chapter on sexuality while holed up in the gypsy wagon on Meibao's land in Taos, captivated by the Anita Hill–Clarence Thomas hearings.

My gratitude to Gilda Frantz for lending me part of the title to chapter 4, "Daughter as Destiny," from her own writing. I received generous assistance from Linda Weidlinger, Bobbie Yow, and Lore Zeller of the C. G. Jung Library in Los Angeles as well as from Charlene Sieg, editor of *Psychological Perspectives*, who helped me find Margaret Ryan. My daughter, Heather Murdock, once again gave me valuable research and editorial assistance and drove from Santa Cruz to Venice to organize my footnotes. My son, Brendan Murdock, gave me insightful feedback on the rewrite and suggestions about illustrations for the book. Ann Glover helped me organize the art, and Christi Albouy helped type the manuscript. I have had the opportunity to participate with two men who have fathered my children: John Murdock, who begat them, and Lucien Wulsin, Jr., who has been a loving stepfather. My deep gratitude to Lucien, my "compassionate rock," for holding a steady course through my storms about absent fathers and supporting me through the final birth throes of this book. My deep appreciation to both Gilda Frantz and Sachico Reece for their wisdom and insights about my personal journey; without Gilda I could not have midwifed this book. My thanks to Ann Levine for first inspiring me to write, and to my teachers, Jean Houston, Joseph Campbell, and Thich Nhat Hanh. My gratitude to my colleagues in the therapeutic community for their insights and wisdom: Linda Olsen Weber,

Flor Fernandez, Alison Acken, and Stephanie Marsten, and to Nancy Rumble and Eric Tingstad for their inspiring music, especially "Big Weather" on *In the Garden*. There are many guardians at the gate who assisted me throughout the writing of this book. You know who you are: Steve, Bev, Adelaide, Polly, Aleph, Judy, Sara, Adele, Henry, Lewin, Lucien Sr., Margaret N., Connie N., Pam, Aimee, my sister Rosemary, and my mother. My grandfather and Uncle Joe fathered me in the best way they knew how by regularly taking me to Yankees games when I was a girl. Of course, I would not have embarked on this task had it not been for my father, a man of enormous creative energy and warm Irish wit, to whom I dedicate this book. Thanks, Matt.

INTRODUCTION

Fathers' Daughters describes the unique psychological complexities of being a "father's daughter," a woman who overidentifies with, or hero-worships, her father. My initial interest in the makings of a father's daughter grew out of my need to understand how being such a daughter has affected my life. In 1990 I wrote *The Heroine's Journey*, a book that describes the psychospiritual development of women. Inspired by a conversation with renowned mythologist Joseph Campbell about his concept of the heroic quest, I formulated a model of development to redefine this quest for women. After the publication of the book, I received hundreds of letters from women all over the world. Many were from fathers' daughters worn out by their efforts to be like men. They commonly reported significant professional and economic success, yet, at the same time, they expressed a deep sense of alienation. They had dutifully followed the rules and guidelines of the patriarchal culture, and, as a result, their inner lives were in disarray. Their overidentification with their fathers and their quests to be like their fathers left them with unanswered questions about how to be comfortable with who they were as women.

I was deeply touched by the common threads of their tales. Each woman conveyed a feeling of exhaustion and depletion as she described in her letter the loss of the feminine side of her nature. One woman who worked in the computer industry spoke for many: "Women who join a high-tech company enter a very masculine model where competition is fierce and the survivors are those in whom the male fighter is strong. Feelings of compassion, understanding, and support are dangerous to one's career. In my ten years of working in Silicon Valley, I have not met one woman who feels good about herself and hasn't abdicated her femininity. As I look back, I am thrilled that I have not turned into a pillar of salt." Although this father's daughter has learned how to function successfully in the male world, her overidentification with father-centered values has deprived her of finding a comfortable center within herself.

A father's daughter is a woman who identifies with her father and imitates men in her pursuit of success. As a little girl, she is a "daddy's girl" who idealizes her father and rejects her mother. She is the apple of her father's eye and receives special treatment and attention from him. She is the envy of her other siblings and, at times, the envy of friends who lack such close relationships with their own fathers. She has her father wrapped around her little finger and knows she can get from him what she wants. As the novelist Jane Smiley wrote about the relationship Caroline, the favorite daughter in *A Thousand Acres*, had with her father: "She was never afraid of him. When she wanted something from him, she just stalked right up to him and asked him for it."

Typically, a father's daughter is the firstborn child or only daughter. But her favored position with her father is not necessarily determined by the order of her birth—it is determined by the intensity of her connection to him. A father's daughter idolizes her father as her hero and wants to be just like him. She emulates his qualities, imitating his walk, tastes, and opinions. She is determined to make him proud.

One woman remembers her feelings about her father when she was an adolescent going to dinner with him alone. She says: "I felt like I was his girl, his date. I felt special. He was definitely my hero during that period. He was incredibly generous, and he always seemed so smart. I could ask him a question about anything and he had read about it. He was boisterous, gregarious, had a dominant personality, and had an opinion about everything. He didn't have a lot of humility. I thought it was great. I soaked it up."

Such a father's daughter is enraptured by her father's perfection and excuses his flaws. She focuses on her mother's flaws instead. She grows up favoring men and male values and often dismisses women as inferior.

This hero worship of the father continues well into adulthood. A thirty-year-old advertising executive puts it this way: "When I think about my father I get this incredible feeling. I realize he has his flaws, and he loses his temper, and sometimes he tries to make decisions for me. But he loves me so much and he's so warm, open, and supportive, I feel really lucky. I just wonder if I appreciate him enough."

There is little doubt that a father's daughter develops her masculine qualities early, emulating her father and the world of men. Her identification with her father gives her a sense of self-confidence and competence in the world, but in her separation from her mother, she also receives a deep wound to the very core of her femaleness. Her relationship to her body, her creativity, her spirituality, and her ability to engage in intimate relationships are all impaired. Most women avoid dealing with issues about their fathers until they are confronted by their own relationship or career problems or by the father's illness or death.

Jungian analyst Marion Woodman writes that not all daughters are fathers' daughters in relation to their personal fathers, but most women are fathers' daughters in relation to the predominant patriarchal culture. Since the rise of contemporary feminism, women have struggled with men and male institutions for equality in the business world, in the home, in academia, and in politics. Yet many women remain unaware of how deeply they continue to reflect their fathers' values. A daughter internalizes her father's view of her, and the more strongly she identifies with him, the more difficulty she has establishing a separate identity of her own.

In writing this book, I have approached the father-daughter relationship from many different vantage points: psychological, mythological, and spiritual. My orientation as a therapist is Jungian with a family-systems background, so the theorists I have included reflect those philosophies. My interest in mythology, fairy tales, and dreams is reflected throughout this book. In Jungian psychology all the characters and parts in a fairy tale or dream are aspects of a single psyche. My hope is that you, as reader, will be able to recognize the characters and landscapes of each dream, myth, and fairy tale as parts of your own psyche.

The most important parts of this book are the modern parables, the stories graciously given to me by other women. I hope that each reader will read their life experiences, as well as my own, in the spirit in which they are offered.* I am sure they will echo memories of your own relationship with your father. For men who read this book, my hope is that you will be better able to nurture your daughters and to understand your wives, sisters, work associates, and clients; and that you will learn something about yourselves.

Writing this book has been a lot like my relationship with my father—love at first sight, and then the rest. After writing the initial outline of the book, I showed it to my friend, Alison, over dinner. Alison and I have been friends for twenty years, exiles from East Coast Irish-Catholic backgrounds. We raised our children together, went to graduate school together while Alison's mother watched the children, and were eventually divorced from our first husbands within one year of each other. We both became teachers of young children and then psychotherapists. Over the years, we swapped stories about our fathers. Alison's alcoholic father had deserted the family when she was twelve. Alison *knew* I still worshipped my father as a hero. She took a long look at the outline for this book, put it down, took a deep breath, and said, "Maureen, do you really want to spend the next three years of your life writing *this*? Don't you realize how painful this is going to be?"

*Names and identities have been changed to preserve the anonymity of clients, group members, workshop participants, and interviewees. Some women chose to reveal their sexual orientation; others did not.

I was taken aback by her remark. Ever the father's daughter, I said, "What are you talking about? It will never take three years, and I think it will be an important book. We've all done the Mother, and now it's time for the Father."

Well, that was four years ago, and I obviously had not done the work Alison had done on her relationship with her father. I ignored Alison's warning (my mother always said, "You're just like your father—you want things your own way!") and continued the process of writing outlines and finally a book proposal. My agent, Beth, sold my book to a "big" publisher in New York, just blocks from my father's advertising agency. I had always wanted to impress my father and win his approval. Certainly *this* would do it!

Little did I know then that completing this book would involve three editors, two rewrites, and three years, or that it would bring me to my knees as I toppled my father (and myself) from his pedestal.

Writing about the father-daughter relationship is like writing a different kind of love story. The rules, constrictions, and taboos are different from those of boy-girl love stories, but it is a love story nonetheless, with a beginning, middle, and end.

Fathers' Daughters also has a beginning, middle, and end. In Part I, we look at the mutual infatuation and identification between daughter and father, and the concurrent exclusion of the mother that leads to an unspoken "covenant" neither father nor daughter understands. In Part II, we explore the sacrifices of creativity, spirituality, and feminine power that a father's daughter makes to fulfill her father's destiny in the world. In Part III, the father's daughter comes to terms with separating her identity from her father. This involves the painful yet vitally necessary step of individuating from him, accepting him as a man, and finding the true beauty, power, and creativity of being a woman.

In her essay "Two for the Price of One," author Sara Maitland writes for each of us who explores this relationship: "I am my father's daughter. I cannot love myself unless I love him."

FATHERS' DAUGHTERS

PART I

Personal Context

Athena by Joanne Battiste.
(Casein, 3 fl × 3 fl in., 1987.
Reprinted by permission of the artist.)

CHAPTER ONE

Fathers' Daughters

Finally I just gave up and became my father. . . .
—Sharon Olds, "Fate"

ONE of the most unexamined relationships today is that which exists between fathers and daughters. It is a relationship laden with expectation and disappointment, admiration and denial, love and abandonment. The manner in which a young girl learns to relate to her father has long-lasting effects on her adult relationships with men as lovers, spouses, friends, bosses, and co-workers. This earliest partnership will also affect her sexuality, creativity, spirituality, and ability to express and manifest her ideas in the world. Left unexamined, the relationship between a daughter and a father will impact her sense of entitlement, power, and authority in her personal life as well as in society.

There are many types of fathering, and each has its own complex issues. The least complicated experience is that of the *good enough father*, who loves his daughter with few or no strings attached and helps her become a self-sufficient woman who can be herself in the company of men.[1] More problematic is the *absent father*, who abandons his daughter through emotional distance, neglect, or death, leaving her feeling vulnerable and longing for his love. The *pampering father* infantilizes his daughter, forever

5

babying her, giving her everything she wants, and ensuring her dependency on him. The *passive father* abdicates his role as provider and guide, leaving his daughter with a lack of respect for authority as she scrambles to figure out everything on her own. The *seductive father* eroticizes his relationship with his daughter and, even if he does not abuse her sexually, binds her to him inappropriately through that unspoken but compelling connection. The *domineering father* demands his daughter's submission and leaves her perpetually fearful and insecure. The *addictive father* uses and abuses his daughter as his addiction dictates, leaving her scrambling for perfection as a shield. Finally, the *idealized father* favors his daughter over his wife and other children and makes his daughter feel special and gifted. This daughter, positioned in the family as her father's favorite, is called a *father's daughter* and, ironically, may have the most difficult time examining the cost of her father's love.

These father-daughter relationships all have emotional consequences, though some are easier to discern than others. The *daughter of an absent father* typically blames herself for her father's abandonment and continually struggles to be "good enough" to win his or another's love. The *pampered daughter* knows she is ill equipped to create a satisfying life for herself and usually finds a father-substitute to take care of her. The *seduced or abused daughter* is continually reminded of her father's violations by her own inner pain, as she searches for a relationship in which she is neither victim nor perpetrator. The *daughter of a passive father* has learned that she can never rely on anyone else and overcompensates throughout her life for her father's lack of authority. The *daughter of a domineering father* is easily bullied into compliance or spends her adult life rebelling, and the *daughter of an addictive father* exhausts herself trying to maintain control over everyone and everything in her life. The *father's daughter* identifies so closely with her father that she has little separate identity of her own. She enters adulthood with such a sense of entitlement and uniqueness that she is rarely motivated to examine the complexities and emotional costs of her relationship with her father. This immensely complex and yet binding relationship between a father's daughter and her father is the focus of this book.

Profile of a Father's Daughter in Adulthood

In my clinical practice, I have found that certain behaviors and characteristics are shared by fathers' daughters as adult women. Because a father's daughter had a strong, positive relationship with her father as a child, as an adult she identifies primarily with him, favors men and male power, and views as secondary the opinions and values of women. During childhood, a father's daughter is her father's confidante, functioning more as a wife than as a daughter. At work, the adult daughter replicates this favored role as the intimate (sexual or not) of a boss. As trusted confidante to the man in power, she maintains the privileged position of favorite daughter but has little power of her own. In this secondary position, fathers' daughters make excellent assistants to "empire builders," CEOs, and those in political power who set out to change the world.

Drawing upon the legacy of her father's favoritism, she feels special and expects to be well received by others. She has high expectations of herself and others, little empathy for limits, and generally won't take no for an answer. She works her body to the limit and won't allow herself to get sick. She has never learned to compromise because she is used to getting her own way, and she therefore encounters difficulties in intimate relationships, which inevitably require skills in listening and negotiation.

A father's daughter seeks to emulate her father at all costs. Adoring him, she internalizes his values and dictates as the inner voice that drives her, demanding that she be productive. As a consequence, a father's daughter is ambitious and responsible in the world of work; she has the focus and determination to achieve her goals and often accepts responsibility for more than she can comfortably handle. She demands perfection from herself and has little tolerance for her own vulnerability. She is considered a success by the standards of a patriarchal, goal-oriented, power-based culture. A father's daughter yearns *to be like* her father and *to be liked by* her father. Sometimes, she actually yearns *to be* her father. She strives not only to know her father's innermost thoughts and feelings but also to experience the type of power and visibility he holds in the world.

Danielle is a clinical social worker who counsels cancer patients and their families. She grew up admiring her father's ability to give counsel to his clients as a small-town lawyer in New England. She spent her early twenties in the Peace Corps in Colombia, where she married a man she thought was like her father.

"I watched my father give comfort to the people of our town, and that value became central for me," says Danielle. "I actually married a man I met in the Peace Corps who I thought had the same values as my father. First I tried to marry a man like my father, and when that marriage didn't work out, I tried to become my father by immersing myself in worthwhile work. He loved his work, and I love mine, too. But I don't know when to stop."

If a daughter is led to identify with her father through his work or his intellect, rather than through his ability to maintain emotional connections, she may conclude that succeeding in the world of work, career, and ideas is the only way to be valued. Some fathers' daughters in their late thirties and forties are pained to realize that they have repeatedly failed at forming intimate relationships, and they grieve the loss of their childbearing years.

Marianne is forty-one years old and an accomplished editor of a professional journal. She enjoyed growing up as the favored child whose father proudly taught her his verbal skills. At the dinner table, she and he held heated debates, from which her mother and sister were excluded by virtue of their inability to compete. Marianne's father trained her to use her mind in a competitive way that has been an asset in her professional life but disastrous for relationships. When she turned forty, she realized that she might never marry.

"I have a strong masculine attitude that is in some ways my nemesis and in some ways my gift. It's my nemesis because men hate it; they find it combative. My unconventional style of femininity threatens them. So much of my identity has been as my father's daughter that many of my boyfriends have said they can't compete with him. I have internalized him to such a degree that they can't be what I expect. I have very little hope of ever getting married."

When a father's daughter goes about the task of finding a mate, her attachment to her father becomes a barrier. She cannot find a mortal man who can live up to her idealized image of her "perfect" father, and she doesn't let anyone get close enough to try. She avoids intimacy by complaining that men don't give her the attention she deserves. Men who don't love her unconditionally, the way she *thinks* her father did, are perceived as not loving her at all.

A father's daughter may idealize her father to such a degree that it is difficult not only to form intimate relationships with other men but also to feel satisfied with her own accomplishments. Idealization of the father makes it impossible for her to value her imperfect talents and contributions to the world. She denigrates her gifts and convinces herself that nothing she does is good enough. She feels distressed that she has not lived up to her father's view of her. This feeling of personal dissatisfaction is like a low-grade virus that never goes away.

"My father had high hopes for me," Marianne reflects. "He told me I could be the first woman president. Part of him believed that I could do anything and that I should do something

really big, because then he would be so proud of me. But there was another part of him that wanted me to be a wife and mother, and that was a much deeper program. So sometimes I think that, no matter what I do professionally to make him proud, I have totally, utterly failed him emotionally because I didn't give him grandchildren."

Marianne is in an impossible bind. The voice she has internalized of her father's expectations gives her no rest. In her effort to please her father, she has still failed him and therefore cannot enjoy what she *has* achieved in her life. When the father is idealized in this way, his daughter becomes dependent upon his approval of her life decisions. Her choices regarding career, spouse, and children often hinge on what she thinks her father would deem acceptable. Her view of what she is entitled to do with her life revolves around her father's superordinate view.

Rejecting the Mother

Central to the experience of being a father's daughter is a rejection of the mother. The reasons for the alliance between father and daughter, and the concurrent exclusion of the mother, are multitudinous. The mother may be depressed, angry, rejecting, powerless, alcoholic, or otherwise emotionally unavailable. A mother may divorce the father or become ill or die early in her daughter's life, thus creating an emotional vacuum that the father tries to fill. Or it may be that the daughter simply prefers her father because they share similar temperaments and interests. Whatever the reason, the mother becomes the "weak link" in the triangle, and the daughter feels profoundly unmothered. Nowhere is this primal triangle more vividly depicted than in the ancient myth of the goddess Athena, patroness of Athens and Greek civilization. Athena is the archetype of the father's daughter in that she is allied with her father in the rejection of her mother.

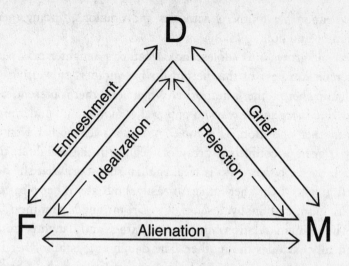

The myth begins with Athena's birth, in which she springs full-grown from her *father's* head, wearing flashing gold armor, holding a sharp spear in one hand, and emitting a mighty war cry. Her father, Zeus, actually *stole* Athena from her mother, Metis, when she was pregnant. Because Zeus feared that Metis would bear a child equal to him in courage and wise counsel, he thwarted fate by tricking his consort into becoming small and swallowing her. With this act, he took away her ability to give birth and stole their daughter for himself. Following her dramatic birth, Athena associated herself only with Zeus, acknowledging him as her sole parent. Though less mythic in stature, this is also what happens to a father's daughter: The mother is metaphorically swallowed by the father as he steals the daughter for himself.

A father's daughter knows at an early age that her father prefers her to her mother. She knows that she is younger, more interesting, and more attentive to her father than her mother is. She knows that she pleases him in a way that her mother never will. To keep her favored position with the father, a father's daughter has to turn away from her mother. She looks forward to spending time with her father, not with her mother. She looks down upon her mother's activities and opinions, finding them feminine and dull.

As she grows into adolescence, a father's daughter may vent the rebelliousness of this period on her mother, subverting or ridiculing her mother's authority. When her father is present, she may find more subtle ways to oppose her mother and undermine her mother's position. This choice of father over mother eventually triggers a conflicting array of feelings in the daughter: triumph over a parent who is weaker than she, scorn that she has been able to "win" her father so easily, guilt about her pleasure in doing so, and finally, a sense of loss regarding her mother.

The intimate relationship between father and daughter automatically excludes the mother. The daughter gets all of her father's attention and secretly feels that she would make a better wife; after all, *she* understands and appreciates him. If the mother is frequently angry, critical, or depressed, it is easy to believe that she is indeed the problem. The father reinforces his daughter's assumptions by comments such as "Your mother just doesn't know how to be happy" or "I don't know how to please her!" The collusion between father and daughter becomes a conspiracy of silent intimacy, which is secret and gratifying but ultimately laden with guilt. The daughter may not become aware of this guilt until she becomes an adult, as Danielle discovered.

Making preparations for her marriage to her Peace Corps colleague in the late 1960s, Danielle went shopping with her mother and father for her wedding dress at Saks Fifth Avenue in New York. Her father had done well professionally and was proud that his graduate-student daughter was engaged to a doctor. But Danielle felt guilty that they were shopping at Saks, knowing that her mother had never enjoyed such an extravagance.

"My father never allowed my mother to practice her profession as a nurse, because he said that her real profession was to be home with the children. She scrimped and saved the whole time we were growing up and shopped for herself at Penney's. My fa-

ther gave her an allowance of ten dollars a week. But by the time I married, my father's financial position was solid.

"I went into Saks looking for a wedding dress and a going-away dress. I fell in love with a raw-silk blue dress that was $250. When I tried it on my father said, 'Take it!' My mother's face fell as she said to me, 'He never bought me anything that was so expensive.' I accepted the gift of the dress, feeling guilty, but what could I say? I feel guilty that we were shopping at Saks, guilty that my mother had had such a difficult life, and guilty that my father had never bought her a beautiful raw-silk dress. I gave her my Phi Beta Kappa key when I graduated and said, 'This is yours.' I wanted her to feel smart, because she had always felt dumb staying home with six kids."

Most wives sense the collusion between husband and daughter and know that, on some level, they are being relegated to an inferior position. They may be unable to admit their own jealousy, or if they try to discuss the collusion with their husbands, they may be told they are "crazy." One woman reported that her mother admitted being very aware of her husband's favoritism toward their daughter but contended that it did not bother her— she was simply glad that the father and daughter had a good relationship. In some situations a wife may actually prefer to be less involved with her husband because of work demands, responsibilities for children, or discordant feelings for her husband. She may also rationalize the father-daughter attachment as a passing phase that is positive for the husband and daughter, if not for her. Whatever the particulars, the favored relationship between father and daughter and its emotional repercussions are rarely discussed or openly acknowledged in any way.

The subtle collusion between daughter and father, with its implicit rejection of the mother, constitutes the initial wounding of the daughter's feminine nature. This wounding impedes or entirely blocks off her receptivity to her intuition, her tolerance of feelings, and her acceptance of the wisdom of her natural body rhythms. In rejecting her mother, the father's daughter rejects herself as a woman. Poet Adrienne Rich writes, "It is a painful fact that a nurturing father, who replaces rather than complements a mother, *must be loved at the mother's expense,* whatever the reasons for the mother's absence."[2]

Only when a father's daughter matures and realizes her complicity in rejecting her mother is she able to feel compassion for this woman of whom she was so critical. Kathleen has not yet reached this stage.

A writer in her early thirties, Kathleen continues to reject her mother in adulthood in order to avoid facing her inability to have an intimate relationship. "I identify with my father because he was a successful writer and he understands the creative process. If I give up my identification with him and with my career, I would have to come to terms with my mother—and that feels like a dark hole. She was always jealous of me. She alternated between being sugary-sweet and downright mean. I learned not to trust women, and I guess I really don't know very much about being comfortable as a woman myself. I'm not ready to come to terms with such major things as mothering and commitment. I know that's why I avoid long-term relationships and still cling to my father."

Kathleen is not yet able to consider the possibility that her mother had valid reasons for her polarized behaviors; it is easier for her to focus on the obvious gifts she received from her father. Such women find that their alliances with their fathers worked to their benefit in establishing their confidence in the world of work but that, in the process, they have denied their needs for attachment and love. Only when they examine their relationships with their fathers will they understand the price they have paid for their favored status.

Difficulties in Examining the Father-Daughter Relationship

Although there are no fixed stages of self-examination for fathers' daughters, I have noticed identifiable patterns across the decades of adult life. A father's daughter is in love with her father well into her twenties. Still his favorite girl, she feels like a traitor if she dares to peer below the surface of her idealized memories. She is fearful of muddying the waters, and even more fearful of losing her father.

In her thirties, a father's daughter may begin to feel anxiety as she reevaluates her cherished view of their relationship and begins to feel the constraints and conditionality of their bond. Still, she denies her anger about her father's interference, controlling behavior, inattention, or the absence of his support in her adult life. Any anger she feels is either internalized or projected onto her husband, mother, siblings, boss, or therapist until it reaches its rightful mark.

A daughter's dawning awareness of what she did not receive from her father, despite the appearance of having received everything, may turn to bitterness and sadness in her forties as she begins to feel her loss—the loss of her mother, the loss of her identity, the loss of her little-girl dreams about what it would be like to be a woman. Some daughters are able to discuss their feelings with their fathers, but most are not. In her fifties and beyond, a father's daughter begins to acknowledge the legacy from her father, both explicitly in her recognition of his teachings and values, and implicitly through her acceptance of his failures and limitations. Each woman finds her own way to heal her pain in her own time. Integration is an ongoing process. Whether or not the father participates in the healing of their relationship, it is the daughter's task to disentangle her identity from his—a task she is loath to undertake.

As a therapist, I have been repeatedly struck by women's reluctance to deal with issues relating to their fathers, despite having ongoing difficulties in the areas of relationships, personal achievement, and creativity. Many fathers' daughters who have worked in depth on their relationships with their mothers dismiss the idea of looking below the surface at their connections with their fathers. Nostalgia, a continuing need to please, and denial of anger obstruct their view. Whether the father was a labor negotiator, a farmer, a truck driver, a doctor, or a tradesman, the father's daughter remains so identified with him that it is difficult for her to evaluate whether his influence on her life has been healthy or intrusive. I often hear comments such as these:

> "My father plays such a large role in my life, it's hard to know where *he* stops and *I* begin."
> "I loved to get his approval so much that I never really knew how *I* felt about the things I was doing to garner that longed-for response in him."
> "He was always my hero. I'll never find anyone like him."
> "My father never allowed himself to be sick, and I have trouble accepting weakness in myself or anyone else."
> "My father worked so hard, and now I'm the same way."

The women who make these comments know that something is amiss as a result of their relationships with their fathers, but they don't want to stir the waters and let that "something" float to the surface, in full view. Most fathers' daughters avoid the "father issue" until their thirties or forties, when they finally begin to realize that their relationship problems or limited career achievements may have something to do with this connection. Or they may be confronted with the shock of his illness or death.

Nostalgia plays a significant role in a woman's refusal to look below the surface. For most fathers' daughters who grew up in "intact families" during the 1940s, 1950s, and 1960s, the time spent with Dad was brief, so they cling to early memories of pleasant times together, or to self-created fantasies about his presence, rather than to painful memories of his absence. But whether her time with her father was brief and infrequent or consistent and regular, a father's daughter *idealizes* her interactions with her father to such a degree that current adult relationships feel flat and inferior in comparison. These cherished memories and fabrications become a measuring stick against which all later relationships are judged.

Most fathers' daughters are raised to please their fathers. Since they are warmly rewarded for this behavior, the impulse to separate from the father remains but a distant pulse. The novelist Mary Gordon writes in *The Writer on Her Work*:

> Bestowing pleasure upon a beloved father is much easier than discovering the joys of solitary achievements. It was easy for me to please my father; and this ease bred in me a desire to please men—a desire for the rewards of a good girl. They are by no means inconsiderable: safety and approval, the warm, incomparable atmosphere created when one pleases a man who has vowed, in his turn, to keep the wolf from the door.[3]

This cozy but unspoken agreement between a father and his daughter in childhood becomes a binding covenant filled with implicit but powerful contingencies. The covenant typically contains subtle, implicit warnings the daughter overlooks as the favored child—warnings such as "Challenge my authority and you'll lose my approval." "Compete with me and you'll lose my protection." "Expose my weakness and I'll leave you forever." As an adult, she may continue to ignore these warnings in exchange for the rewards.

Gerry, a twenty-eight-year-old single woman who is building a career as a graphic artist, talks about how difficult it is to separate from her father because he still provides for her materially in a way she believes she cannot do for herself. "I don't want to be too critical of my father because he just helped me buy a new car. I know that he gives me too much attention—but I don't have anyone else in my life now who is sending me valentines, so I don't want to give it up."

A father's daughter may rail in protest against the injustices of patriarchal institutions, but she will protect her own father at all costs from her buried anger. One woman said, "I don't want to feel anger toward my father because, no matter what he did—and I know that some of his behavior was unacceptable—I *understand* him. I want to continue to love him and be his daughter, and being angry negates that love." Such a simplistic attitude keeps her a child, emotionally. When a father's daughter is finally motivated to examine her father's influence on her life, she may be surprised and even shocked at the extent to which her thoughts, feelings, wishes, values, and behavior are motivated by an underlying desire to please him, to reflect him. I know that I was shocked to my core.

For as long as I can remember, my mother and my parents' friends told me. "You're just like your father—you are your *father's daughter*." I didn't know what that meant because, as a child, I didn't look anything like my father, nor did I have his abilities. I had my mother's dark hair and hazel eyes, not my father's fair hair and blue eyes; and I couldn't draw like him, which is what I most wanted to do. I took great pride in their assessment, however, because I *wanted* to be like him.

As a young girl I saw my father as nothing less than a god; most young girls do. He was funny, attractive, creative, and strong; he was intelligent and dynamic; and, as the CEO of an advertising agency, he had power. He was ambitious and worked hard to make his agency successful. I couldn't wait for him to come home from work; I wanted to please him and make him proud by reporting my daily accomplishments. Both consciously and unconsciously, I chose my father over my mother, and silently he approved my choice. He became my ally and I, his.

During adolescence, I sensed that my father preferred me to my mother and my sister (who was nine years younger). I was thrilled to be my father's favorite; he was attentive to me, and I soaked up his attention. I was interested in everything he had to say. I wanted to hear about his work, his ideas, his clients. My mother didn't have the time to be so enraptured. She was a home-maker; she had to cook, clean, iron his shirts, and carpool. If anything, my mother was indifferent and sometimes hostile to my father's accomplishments. Because I didn't know that he had refused to support her desire to become a decorator, she seemed unduly negative to me. I thought she just didn't appreciate all he did to provide for us. I had a false sense of power because I allied myself with my father, who held the power in the family. Secretly I began to look down upon my mother, seeing her as ordinary. But I hid these feelings for fear of hurting her or incurring her wrath.

Throughout my adolesence and early adulthood, it never occurred to me that my actions, values, and attitudes were modeled after my father's and were geared for his approbation. It wasn't until my late thirties and early forties, after I had raised my own children and established my career as a writer and psychotherapist, that I gradually came to realize I was still hungering for my father's attention. Much of my desire to be successful in the world reflected more my need for his approval than my own inner desires.

Although I did not follow him into advertising, other aspects of my life became vehicles for obtaining his praise and approval. I wrote for publication, gave workshops around the country, and took satisfaction from seeing my work in print. I became what author Signe Hammer describes in *Passionate Attachments* as a "desperate achiever" who works for love. Such a woman wants to be the focus of her father's pride and unconsciously designs her life as an extension of his to gain his attention.

I have always regarded the world of art as my father's realm. At age forty, I entered art school part-time, supposedly to improve my skill as a photographer. The underlying reality was that my father had never acknowledged my talent as an artist and I wanted to prove to myself (and to him) that he was wrong. Within the first semester I discovered that constant negative critiques about my photographs of "ritual spaces" in nature did nothing to nurture my creative process, and I withdrew from school. When I reviewed my motivations for entering art school, it occurred to me for the first time that I had really been seeking my father's approval to validate my creativity. Art school had replaced my dad. I also realized that I was competing with my father for *his* attention—not with my mother or my sister, but with my father himself.

This thought stunned me. I started to feel silly, worthless, and finally sad. It was humiliating to realize that I had spent forty years jumping up and down (metaphorically), saying, "Look at me, look at me!" and that I could never really get the sustained attention or approval I sought. I wasn't as interesting to him as he was to himself! I recognized then how much my need to achieve was driven by a desire for his love. I must have decided at an early age that my very survival depended upon him and that to be favored and loved, I had to perform in a particular way. Barring that, I was on my own.

A father's daughter is phobically afraid of hurting her father's feelings because she is terrified of losing his love—and one is equated with the other. Indeed, she goes numb at the prospect of confronting him, fearing that if they disagree or she refuses to remain allied with him, he'll withdraw his love or, worse, express his wrath. Some daughters even believe that such a confrontation would cause the father's death. The fear of his loss prevents them from attempting any truthful communication.

When I began to write this book, I had a powerful dream about my father dying. It was so real and painful that I didn't want to continue with the project. The threat of his death was almost too much to bear. If I did proceed, then on some level my father would die. Here is a portion of the dream as I recorded it in my journal:

My father has died and I am bereft. I go to my mother to tell her that Dad has died, but she is not interested. She has to go to their new house site in Florida to oversee the construction. She acts as if his death is no big deal. I turn to my daughter to talk to her about it, but she doesn't want to feel my pain and she leaves. I try to phone my friend, Pauline, whose father died when she was thirteen, but she has moved to Kansas and I cannot reach her. There is no one around for me to talk to about my father's death and I feel lost. I think about how I will have no one to celebrate this Father's Day [with], and I realize that I've always taken his presence for granted.

It took me a long time to wake up from this dream and to understand that, indeed, it was a dream, not reality. At first I was disoriented as I tried to shake off the dreaded feelings. I thought about how my father had always been my main parent, my main support, the parent to whom I told my secrets, the parent who listened. Without him, there would be no one to hear me. If he died, part of me would die, too.

In the dream, my mother doesn't care about my feelings over my father's death. She is inured to my grief and busy doing her own work overseeing the building of a new house. She is finally free to do what she has always wanted to do. I turn to my daughter, but her boundaries are clear; she's at a point in her life where the world is open to her, and she doesn't want to carry my pain. I try to find my friend who knows what it's like to lose a father, but she has moved to the heartland and I cannot reach her. I feel terribly alone, bereft without my father. There is no one to comfort me, and I feel like a child.

The dream stopped me cold. It sounded a siren indicating that I was entering forbidden territory. What taboo was I breaking in talking about the father-daughter relationship? Did I really want to look below the surface of the collective nostalgia celebrated on Father's Day? Would my words destroy our relationship or, worse, cause my father's death? I was gripped with terror at the thought of no longer being my father's favorite, at the idea that I could even be the instrument of his death. Even if that death were only symbolic, I shuddered at the void such a death would leave in me. I also knew that I would not be able to get on with my own life until I came to terms with this powerful and primal connection.

CHAPTER TWO

Personal Identity:
What It Means to Be a
Father's Daughter

We turn to our Daddy in our bid for independence, autonomy, self-hood—and, too often, our bid stops short, right
there in Daddy's lap. He's not the bridge out into the world,
he is the world.

—Signe Hammer, *Passionate Attachments*

The dreams of fathers are hard. They want daughters in their
own image, to embody masculine prowess, achievement, independence. For many women, to do "well" in public terms is
the only way they can hope to attract his attention.

—Olivia Harris, "Heavenly Father"

A FATHER is clearly different from a mother, and the perception of this difference helps the daughter differentiate herself
from her mother. Studies by Dr. T. Berry Brazelton at Harvard
have shown that at an age as early as six months, a baby girl will
respond differently to her father's voice and body than she will
to her mother's.[1] A daughter gets her cues from her father about
whether or not it is good to be female—and, even more, what it
means to be female—by observing his interactions with her
mother as well as her own interactions with him. His attitude to-

ward his daughter's femaleness in part determines whether she develops a healthy or crippling sense of self.

The daughter assimilates a particular understanding about what it means to be female by observing what qualities please her father. A father can convey that he loves his daughter only when she is strong, capable, and independent, or only when she is obedient, docile, and charming, or only when she is busy and productive; or he can convey that his love is strictly dependent on her singular attachment to him. One way or another, the daughter learns what is considered "good" by the father, and if she is a father's daughter, she strives to meet his implicit criteria with all her might. Her ongoing desire to please her father will affect her ability to cope with issues of attachment and autonomy for the rest of her life.

Good Girls

Within the first few months of life most daughters learn that being a "good girl" is more rewarding than being bad. Good girls learn to be quiet, obedient, dependable, and loyal; in exchange, they are caressed and hugged and get their fathers' attention. As little girls, they have already learned how to listen, make eye contact, sparkle, smile, and nod in agreement. In short, they know how to make their daddies happy.

A father cultivates his daughter's compliance by encouraging her to be affectionate, agreeable, and self-sacrificing. She is rewarded for having an easy temperament and for keeping peace in the family. She is eager to please. Even at a very young age, she learns how to live out her father's ideal of the perfect female. She rarely argues with him except within the parameters he specifies; she disagrees with her mother instead.

A good girl rarely breaks rules or lies; if she does, she makes sure she doesn't get caught. In school, she is a good student and turns in assignments on time. If her father reinforces her intellectual development at home, she is quite vocal in school. If, however, she is given the message that good girls should be seen but not heard, she will rarely speak up in class unless called upon, rarely ask questions, or differ with the teacher.

As an adult, the father's daughter who was a "good girl" finds that her compliance keeps her invisible and inaudible. She feels like a child. She doesn't want to stand out or be subject to scrutiny or criticism. She has difficulty finding her voice because she has been listening most of her life or repeating her father's opinions. She would like to remove the facade of compliance but fears the isolation that might result if she no longer performs as expected. Although her continued silence and submission make her sad, an accommodating smile is securely frozen on her face.

Bad Girls

Bad girls—daughters who are disobedient, rebellious, confrontational, loud, or precociously sexual—are usually rejected for being too much to handle. However, if the father is a man who flouts convention, who values "spunk" or even rebellion, the daughter will be rewarded for being a bad girl. If he breaks rules, she may too. Such a father supports his daughter's fearlessness, contrariness, and high spirits, giving her a secret nod when she confronts authority—particularly when she stands up to her mother.

As a young father's daughter, I learned to identify with my father's role as the rebellious one in the family. My father liked to see himself as a bad boy who got away with mischievous but harmless acts. He told hilarious stories about forging weekend passes for himself and his buddies during his years in the service. He was always "in trouble" with my mother. She played "the heavy" in the family, the strict disciplinarian and disapproving mother, and he acted out the role of the naughty boy.

Since my father liked breaking rules, and since I identified so closely with him, I was encouraged (though not directly, of course) to break rules too. It was okay to be bad; in fact, it was *preferable*. And it felt exhilarating. He always said that the people who were the most interesting, creative, and fun to be with were "a little bad." But not too bad. The acceptable degree of badness remained undefined until I got into trouble with my mother in my early twenties, when I came home from college a graduate, but unwed and pregnant—a major transgression in an Irish-Catholic family. Although I married shortly thereafter, my mother unleashed her anger upon me while my father stood by silent and helpless. He did not intervene between my mother and me; nor did he defend me. He let me fend for myself. I was stunned by his mute response. My father never carried the moral outrage in the family, and although I realized that most fathers do not welcome a daughter's unwed pregnancy, I had expected my father's support. After all, he had always accepted my secrets and tolerated my mistakes. His silence indicated his disapproval, and his refusal to protect me from my mother felt like a betrayal.

Family therapist Betty Carter writes that when a daughter identifies with her father in alliance against her mother, she stands up to her mother in a way that her father never does. She knows that her conflicts with her mother don't really upset her father. He secretly encourages them. However, what the daughter does not understand is her parents' unspoken but compelling mutual dependency. If her mother gets so upset that it causes a problem for the father, he will join with his wife to let his daughter know that she has stepped over the line.[2] My father's emotional withdrawal was an indication that I had crossed that boundary, and I felt abandoned by him. A father's daughter who takes for granted her preferred position with her father is jolted into examining this cherished assumption when her father finally aligns himself with his wife.

In the following example, Pam discovered that not only has she emulated her father's outrageous behavior, but she also has consistently chosen unconventional men. Unfortunately, bad boys do not make dependable partners.

Pam is a forty-three-year-old administrator of a nonprofit social services agency. She is a self-proclaimed father's daughter who has always identified with her father's mischievous behavior. As a child, she listened raptly to his tales about the escapades he shared growing up with a group of friends called the "Never Sweats," who were naughty and fun. Nothing ever bothered them. She says, "I naturally identified with that. I was the one most like my father, naughty and extroverted. Any time he said, 'Don't you dare,' that was the best challenge for me."

Pam proved her naughtiness when she started dating her father's married business partner immediately after her father's death. She suspected that her father had known of her attraction to his partner, but she had refrained from initiating a relationship while her father was alive. She says she could almost hear her father say, "You waited until I died, you creep." She responded, "Yup, I did." She loved that part of it.

For Pam, men have been no more than a source of entertainment; since her divorce in her late twenties, she has never been interested in any kind of ongoing commitment. Her degree of identification with the mischievous aspects of her father's behavior has completely circumscribed and limited the range of her relationships.

The Role of Gender in Identity

Before we examine those aspects of emotional development that are unique to a father's daughter, we need to consider the larger social issue of how gender differences impact emotional development in general. In most households, girl children are considered to be more sensitive and are therefore allowed to cry and feel fear, whereas boys may be given more leeway to express anger or aggression. Current studies by Jean Berko Gleason and her Boston University colleagues have shown that parents reinforce certain stereotypical expectations of boys and girls by applying different linguistic standards to each sex. They speak in softer tones with girls, tempering their expression of negative feelings. They are more assertive and direct with boys. For example, a father might say to a son, "Cut that out!" whereas with a daughter he might say, "It's okay, sweetie; now let's look at that tiny bug over there."[3] In this way, a daughter learns that direct, assertive communication is associated with males and that indirect, diversionary communication goes along with being female.

Daughters discover that for girls, acceptable feelings are of the positive, loving variety. Being affectionate, grateful, satisfied, quiet, content, happy, compliant, and conciliatory will usually win a father's (as well as a mother's) approval, if not his love. Daughters who express too much sadness, anger, defiance, fear, sensuality, or aggression quickly learn that their feelings are unacceptable. Such a daughter is seen as "difficult."

Most men who are fathers today grew up in an era in which the expression of feelings was unacceptable for male children. A boy was not allowed to cry, show fear, express uncertainty, or exalt in joy. Caught in fear, pain, or sadness, a little boy was told to "act like a man," "tough it out," or "grin and bear it." He learned to mask pain with performance, fear with machismo, and loneliness with activity. He also learned to swallow his joy. He learned always to have an answer in the face of uncertainty and to conceal sadness with humor or rage. It is little wonder, then, that many fathers have such a hard time accepting emotions.

If a father is not connected to his own feelings, he can't hear and empathize with those his daughter expresses. He defends against them instead. If, for example, he is threatened by his own feelings of sadness, he may belittle, tease, ignore, or distract his daughter with a story when she cries. He may tell her to get the "crying towel" or go to her room. She learns that it is not safe to express her feelings around her father; they will not be heard.

This dynamic becomes intensified for a father's daughter. Because her father identifies so strongly with her, a father's daughter is not allowed to experience or express emotions that he deems undesirable. Her father actually tries to control her feelings—such as anger, sadness, fear, and uncertainty—by extinguishing them with rational arguments. When she is rejected by friends, he will say, "Don't be sad, honey; those girls don't know anything." When she is angry at her friends, he will say, "Don't waste your time with those idiots. Get on with it." When she feels fear about the future, he will say, "Don't worry about the future, sweetheart; you can do anything." Her feelings are neither explored nor assuaged; she learns to hide them, feeling alone and isolated, or she pretends that nothing hurts. The unheard, unacceptable feelings do not go away, however. They collect in dark corners of her personality and eventually take on a life of their own.[4]

When a girl repeatedly swallows her feelings, certain behaviors become entrenched. She becomes expert at denial, second-guessing, repression, or rebellion. As an adult, she numbs her feelings with work, alcohol, food, or sex; that way, she doesn't have to experience pain or confusion. She consults friends about whether her feelings are valid by asking, "How would you feel in this situation?" She expresses hurt with an extended pout or slow-burning resentment. She projects her disowned anger onto others by blaming them for failed relationships.

A father's daughter gets the strong message that not only must she protect her father from *her* uncomfortable feelings, but she is also responsible for *his* feelings. She must never let him feel sad or angry, defeated or disappointed; she absorbs his anxiety and grief—particularly about his relationship with his wife, her mother; she protects him from his bad feelings by listening, cajoling, consoling, or trying to be perfect. She feels miserable if she lets him down, and she unconsciously learns to compensate for his unexpressed emotions.

I discovered that my father's discomfort with his unexpressed grief over the death of his own father made it imperative for me to assuage his sense of loss. My grandfather died when my father was thirteen. My father immediately went to work to support his mother, older brother, and younger sister. He became the man of the family. He attended a trade high school, where he alternated work one week and school the next. After high school graduation, he worked full-time from the age of seventeen all the way to seventy. He has repeatedly told me that "there was never time to play" and so he never learned how. He didn't feel that he could take time off as an adult to learn tennis or golf, and now that he is finally retired, he feels handicapped in his efforts to join other men in these activities. His sense of responsibility fueled his work; his isolation fueled his productivity. Work provided him great satisfaction but left little room for dealing with feelings.

I remember as a child feeling an aching sadness for my father every time he showed me his father's golden pocket watch. He had been a boy without a father, and now he was a father without a son. He talked about his father with pride and admiration, never showing any sadness, but I could sense the depth of his loss. Not having a son of his own somehow intensified the loss of his father. It became very important to me to make it up to him by never letting him feel sad or lonely and by acting "tough" like a boy. He wouldn't tolerate the expression of "female" feelings like weakness or fear. When I tried to tell him about my difficulty coping with my mother's anger, he always told me to "rise above it" and "learn to be patient." There was no outlet for my pain. My father was a good teacher. I learned from his example to fill loneliness and vulnerability with productivity—the culturally acceptable male opiate.

Mirroring the Father's
Feeling Style

What the father's daughter learns to do with her emotions as a child determines how she functions emotionally as an adult. Most fathers' daughters mirror the feeling style of their fathers as adults themselves, masking vulnerability with anger, fear with machismo, and loneliness with workaholism. They have learned how to fill their emptiness with activity, how to perform rather than feel. They have learned to deny their vulnerability rather than accept their limitations. They have learned to ignore their health.

Thirty-one-year-old Nancy is a father's daughter who learned that her father would not tolerate her sad feelings but approved of her anger. He could do something with her anger; he could argue with it. Nancy never saw her father express sadness or uncertainty, and when she felt sad he would tell her, "I don't want to hear it! Go to your room and shut the door." Because he couldn't bear to see her vulnerability, he abandoned her emotionally. If she was angry, however, it was a different story. "Anger was okay because we could rationally fight about it," Nancy recalls. "Sadness was infantile, and he would have no part of it."

Nancy's father, a lawyer, died when she was only eleven. Early on, she decided to follow him into law. She has found that most men in her law firm replicate the feeling style of her father in their combativeness and rigid certainty.

"The guys at my law firm are never sad or uncertain; they have the answers to everything, and their way of dealing with sadness is to be angry. They're angry a lot. So I'm in an environment that promotes not being sad and accepts anger and fighting as a way of dealing with people. And always being certain—you never admit as a lawyer that you don't know. I do, but they don't."

Nancy confronted the feeling style of her father by choosing a work environment where she is surrounded by similar men. In an effort to sort out her own style of emotional expression, she first had to come to terms with her father's. Nancy's father was comfortable with anger, and that's what she learned to express. She has since decided to explore the full range of her identity and is pursuing her desire to write as one way of reaching her long-buried emotions.

Whereas Nancy's father sublimated his feelings with anger, Luella's father used work to obliterate his feelings. Luella, an artist in her early forties, has had to make a concerted effort not to let busyness consume her life.

Luella's father was a "good ol' boy" from the South who had been a fighter pilot in the Philippines during World War II. He was a legendary Clint Eastwood look-alike who conducted himself as if he were always on a mission. He brought an element of reckless endangerment to all situations, and no one questioned his actions. Luella was his "first lieutenant," completely upholding his value system. His priority in life was to remain active; he valued busyness, productivity, and concrete projects. He worked from dawn till dusk as a builder/developer and spent his free time working his farm. Luella dutifully emulated him, working long hours at an advertising agency by convincing herself that everyone was dependent on her productivity (her mission). Her workaholism resulted in psychosomatic symptoms which eventually led her to seek therapy. As she began to explore her relationship with her father, Luella recalled the following experience:

"The most emotional moment I ever exchanged with him was when I was twenty-six. Until then, I had been his mirror image, upholding his work ethic by driving myself as hard as he did. That Thanksgiving, I took my dog and my two younger sisters up to my father's farm, which was outside town away from the family house.

"My father had left strychnine out at the farm for a bear or

fox that had been rummaging through the garbage. He had forgotten to tell me about the poisoned meat and there was no phone at the farm, so he couldn't warn me. Of course, you know what happened. My dog died, and a neighbor, Mr. Coleman, and I buried the dog. Mr. Coleman hated my father and took this opportunity to vent his rage at my father's irresponsibility. But I felt very protective of my father. When I got home, I was shocked to find him standing in the driveway, sobbing, telling me he loved me."

That was the first time Luella had ever seen her father cry, and it was also the first time she had had to pay a price for his actions. The death of her dog affected her profoundly, and she began to question her father's mode of operation. Everything he did took on a sense of urgency, and she had been just as compulsive in living her life. She had spent her twenties and thirties masking her feelings with alcohol and overwork, and it was only after her father's death that she finally felt free to experience a broad range of emotions. She had idealized him to such a degree in her childhood and adolescence that she felt she was keeping him alive by emulating his actions.

Emotional Expression in the Father-Daughter-Mother Triangle

In the triangle that exists between a father's daughter, her father, and her mother, the mother is typically emotionally unavailable or emotionally unappealing to the father/husband. She may be depressed, ill, angry, cold and remote, busy, nervous, or powerless. The daughter identifies with her father, who is seen as the "easier" parent, the better parent, whom she chooses to emulate. She makes a decision to be *nothing* like her mother.

Since most fathers do not express emotions (other than delight or anger), their wives are left to carry their unexpressed "shadow" feelings such as depression, disappointment, anxiety, and grief. The husbands project these unexpressed feelings onto their wives. In any family, relationship, or group, when one person acts out or manifests a certain set of feelings, the other people in the relationship feel far less need to express those same feelings. For example, when a mother is anxious about her safety in a particular situation, other members of the family, who may indeed share the same anxiety for themselves, deny their own feelings to take care of or ridicule her. In this way they project their own unacceptable feelings of anxiety onto her. Each member of the family is "allotted" certain feelings they are allowed to express. A son may be angry and sullen, whereas a daughter is expected to be bright and helpful. If the father dominates the family, he will greatly influence who gets to express what feelings.

When a daughter allies herself with her father, she rejects the unacceptable feelings in herself that are expressed by her mother. She splits off from her own grief, anger, fear, and loneliness. Finding her mother's "negative" feelings repulsive, she curtails her own capacity to experience and express any negativity. The father is seen as light (free of negative feelings), innocent, and superior, while the mother is left to carry the dark (unacceptable) feelings and is therefore sullied and inferior.

In the following examples we will see how the contrast between the idealized fathers and the mothers who are viewed as depressed, angry, envious, or passive impacts the father's daughter. In each example, the daughter allies with her father, internalizing his feeling style while repudiating her mother's.

THE DEPRESSED MOTHER

When a mother is depressed, the father often expresses more Pollyanna-like feelings. He may patronize his wife's moods in an effort to lift her depression. He may encourage his daughter to "be considerate" and "helpful" to Mother, because of her problems (a wink of the eye may accompany the instruction, conveying the inferiority of the mother in relation to the very capable husband and daughter). The daughter learns to be nice, but she can't *stand* her mother.

Danielle is an attractive and energetic woman in her early fifties who could easily pass for forty. She has raised four children and exudes positive feelings to family and friends as well as to the cancer patients with whom she works as a clinical social worker. She grew up in the Northeast and has a strong Yankee work ethic. Her mother was a homemaker who raised six children (four girls and two boys). In comparison, her father, a lawyer, had the privilege to come and go as he pleased.

Danielle describes her family as being like a jalopy that would periodically break down. "Actually, my mother was the jalopy, my father was the driver, and I was in the front seat. The rest of the kids were in the backseat, playing around. The jalopy would break down when Mom became physically ill or depressed, and everyone had to stop whatever we were doing and tend to Mother. Her needs became paramount. She was the only one who could express negative feelings and letdown. Dad dutifully took care of her, and the rest of us learned to be self-sufficient. I identified with Dad, who was nice, affable, gregarious, and who only encouraged happy feelings and never expressed negative ones. In fact, I never saw him sad except the day his mother died. Mom acted out all the negative feelings in our family; she was consumed by them.

"My father was clearly the more attractive parent; he always wore a bow tie, always looked dapper and neat. He was a professional in a small town. Contrast this dashing figure who smelled like Old Spice with my mother, who wore ankle socks and Oxford shoes and did the whole charwoman thing to the hilt. She was oppressed and depressed. To ally with her would have been to ally with negativity, sadness, and death, whereas Dad would come home full of energy. He worked over a bakery so his arms were always filled with baked goods.

"It is only now, in my fifties, that I'm beginning to appreciate *the energy anger can bring. I've made a commitment to find my own voice. I'm beginning to feel anger toward my father. I started to realize how deceptive his happy-go-lucky attitude really was; he was actually in control of my mother. I see now that he wouldn't allow her to continue to work as a nurse, which was her profession. She was deprived of anything that would bring her some sense of self-esteem. They were both caught in the culture of the times. Now I see my mother as a tragic figure and a victim of circumstances."*

Danielle learned to be nice and affable like her father; above all else, she did not want to be like her mother. To this day, she feels insecure when she's not agreeable. Her mother was ignored or placated by her children, and Danielle is afraid that if she is not "nice enough," she too will be abandoned. She did not examine the origin of her "good girl" feeling style until she realized she had married a man who was always angry in order to avoid expressing any negative feelings herself. Her divorce helped her find her own voice.

THE ANGRY, JEALOUS MOTHER

Many mothers of previous generations had little power in society and felt ignored by their husbands and rejected by their daughters. They became angry at their lack of status and control in the family and society and envious of their daughter's favored position and potential. In part, their anger contributed to the emergence of the women's movement: Fathers' daughters who had angry, jealous mothers vowed to be nothing like them, by achieving the power that their fathers held.

In the following example, the mother had two formidable rivals for her husband's affection: her daughter and her mother-in-law, both of whom incited jealousy and anger in her. The daughter learned to manipulate the rivalry between the two adult women in order to lure her father away from her mother.

Elizabeth is a banker by day and a comedienne at night. She was a beautiful, articulate only child with long blonde hair. She grew up the pampered daughter of an attractive, charismatic diplomat who was stationed abroad. From the time she was very young, her father lavished attention on her while ignoring his wife. Elizabeth emulated her father by disregarding her mother, often refusing to obey her, and then acted like the perfect lady with her father. Mother and daughter became bitter enemies early on. Whenever her mother said, "Just wait until your father comes home," Elizabeth would eagerly await him in her room. When he appeared, she regularly persuaded him to go for a walk, whereupon she would entertain him with stories about her friends and minimize her mother's grievances. Her father encouraged their alliance by never taking her mother's complaints seriously. He would just wink at Elizabeth. The mother saw this collusion and felt both demeaned and enraged.

Elizabeth's grandmother greatly exacerbated the situation by encouraging her rebellion against her mother. Grandmother always felt that Elizabeth's mother had stolen her favorite son away from her. Elizabeth says, "She used to say how wonderful it would be if we could get Daddy back from the 'dragon lady.' " Elizabeth learned early how to manipulate others, just as she had been used in the emotional drama among these adults. As a consequence, Elizabeth's identity as an adult is limited by her self-centered focus, her need to have her own way, and her inability to compromise in relationships.

With a background as a math major at Harvard, Elizabeth uses principles of geometry to describe the triangle she experienced with her mother and father. She says, "Triangles are constituted by three points. My father, who was larger than life to me, was one point, and then tangent to him, actually touching, was me, the chip off the old block. On the other side, which would be a straight line because a three-pointed triangle can be a straight line, was my mother. She was directly across from my father at a great distance."

Unfortunately, Elizabeth's insight remains theoretical. She has been unwilling to give up her idealized image of her father and is therefore unable to explore her own emotions. In her early thirties, Elizabeth has had two failed marriages and makes herself unavailable for close female friendships. Such a father's daughter sees women as negative and ineffectual and remains adept at manipulating men to get what she wants. She will remain tied to Daddy in his misogyny. Betty Carter writes that such a daughter "will grow old but will never grow up."[5]

THE PASSIVE MOTHER

In the preceding profiles, the fathers were generally perceived as attractive, positive members of the family. They welcomed their daughters' affections and were idolized by them in return. Now we will look at the critical, controlling father and husband whose wife reacts with passivity.

This father usually exempts his favorite daughter from the kind of aggressive control with which he treats his wife and other children. The father's daughter is at first immune to her father's anger and perceives her mother as being the one at fault. She sees her mother as weak and ineffective, resents her passivity, and becomes highly critical of her and females in general. Given her favored status with her father, the father's daughter will never identify with her mother, choosing instead her father, who has the power. She may even internalize some of the ruthless characteristics her father displays or lash out at her mother, other family members, and friends. Rather than confronting a controlling father about his anger, a father's daughter learns to placate him, thus helping to keep his power intact.

In the following example, the father's anger was directed primarily at his wife, who coped by escaping into alcoholism. Her daughter, although apparently aligned with her father throughout childhood, nonetheless internalized his mistreatment of her mother and later turned it on herself.

Lauren is a thirty-nine-year-old nurse who identifies herself as a father's daughter even though her father was a tyrant. A prominent doctor in their suburban community, he secretly controlled his family with his anger. Hearing the garage door go up at night sent each member bolting to various ends of the house. Even Lauren's autistic brother responded to the sound of the garage door by hiding. As other family members dispersed, Lauren met her father at the door and tried to soothe his frayed nerves.

"Mom would drink because she couldn't stand him coming home," Lauren said. "He would yell about everything. Nothing we did pleased him. I was the only one who could calm him, but that, too, was short-lived.

"My father always complained about my mother's drinking, but he never really wanted her to stop. He berated her to be a strong person like the neighborhood wives who had 'well-managed' lives. Yet he poured her a drink every night before he poured his own. Then he got all bent out of shape when she got sloppy and blamed her for being weak and ineffective. If she stopped drinking, she would have her own life. But he would much rather have her weak because then he had power."

Lauren has never been able to express her resentment toward her father, and only in adulthood does she feel protective of her mother. Decades of resentment have turned to sadness. She has been sad for a long time. She cannot get angry in any situation and has been a caretaker her whole life. Instead of seeking to meet her own needs, she keeps herself safe by giving to others. Her friends tell her that she confuses loving with giving. She is unmarried and treats the men in her life like brothers.

Lauren has internalized her father's controlling voice; she is tyrannical toward herself, demanding perfection, and has difficulty separating from her father's disapproval. She wants to pursue studies in acupuncture, but her father constantly criticizes her interest in alternative medicine. He demeans any approach outside his sphere of knowledge. She finds herself doubting her choices and struggles to assert herself with the doctors at the hospital where she works.

She says, "It's hard for me to stand up for what I believe in when someone discounts it. This goes back to my father. Every doctor who belittles what I want to do at the hospital is my father. It's not just somebody. It's somebody very powerful."

Fear of her father's disapproval and anger mutes Lauren's voice even in her dreams. When she began to examine her relationship with her father in therapy, she had the following dream:

> I am visiting my parents for the holidays and give birth in my father's house. It is so real—the gush of warm blood, the slippery feel, the muscular cord still attached. I lay there feeling the baby, thinking it must be too young to survive, since I hadn't really been pregnant. I am worried that the sheets are covered with blood, but I figure I can hide them from my father. The baby isn't moving, and I finally get the courage to pick it up and look at it. It is a baby girl, perfectly formed, all clean and dressed in a little shirt and diaper. But she is blue. As soon as I look at the baby, she turns pink, opens her eyes, and starts to cry as if she is suddenly beginning life. I am seized by overwhelming, sickening panic that my father will hear her. Without even thinking, I gently place my thumb over the baby's mouth to quiet her and, in an instant, all life disappears. She turns blue and dies.

In the dream, Lauren gives birth to her own identity, and the thought that her father might find out sends her into a panic. She silences the baby and, in doing so, kills her. She says, "I killed the baby so my father wouldn't find out. And I thought I was safe from his domination by living three thousand miles away." Like many other fathers' daughters, Lauren has internalized her father's voice to such a degree that it prevents her from meeting her core needs.

In each of these relationships the father plays the dominant role in determining the emotional range of the family, while the mother remains ineffective. Each daughter allies with her father and distances herself from her mother. By now it should be clear that there is not just one type of father or father's daughter. It is important to keep this in mind as you read this book. Fathers' daughters develop a wide variety of behavioral and emotional responses as a result of overidentifying with their fathers, although, *in general*, they commonly deny their own feelings.

Danielle's father was seen as positive and attractive and her mother as either angry or depressed. Danielle learned to express only those pleasant feelings with which her father was comfortable, and she still struggles to cope with darker feelings like anger and grief. At fifty-three, she is just beginning to express the full range of her self-identity.

Elizabeth's father was a charismatic man with political and financial power, around whom his mother, wife, and only daughter revolved. Elizabeth learned how to manipulate her father and eclipse her mother. She learned the right thing to say to keep a man's attention and, to this day, jealousy guards her position around other women.

Lauren's father controlled the family with his anger, and her alcoholic mother was powerless to confront him. He was a dangerous force which Lauren learned to appease. To survive, she became a "good girl," silencing her feelings along with her wants and needs. Her liberation will come about only if she can release her identification with her father and his disapproval to choose her own life.

Each daughter has a different behavioral response to her father, who is the pivotal point of her attention. She may become nice, manipulative, a workaholic, or a caretaker—but in each situation the father's daughter learns *which feelings to express and which to deny or repress*. The development of her identity is therefore limited by the range of feelings her father allows her to experience.

He Keeps the Key by Joanne Battiste.
(Oil, 40 × 36 in., 1991.
Reprinted by permission of the artist.)

CHAPTER THREE

Fathers' Daughters and Sexuality

Fathers are supposed to teach their daughters how to be women, that is, how to love men and serve them and use them, coexist with them, how to desire them in a seemly manner. A good father domesticates his daughter, so that when she is twenty or so he can hand her over, polished to a high gloss, to another man. But my father refused to do that. Perhaps he never intended to hand me over to another man.
—Shirley Abbott, *The Bookmaker's Daughter*

It is not mothers who free women from their fathers. They leave their daughters as yet unawakened.
—Carolyn G. Helibrun, *Writing a Woman's Life*

A DAUGHTER learns about many aspects of femininity from her interactions with her father. How she feels about her sexuality, how she behaves in the company of males, and what she expects from males derives in large part from her interactions with her father. She learns how to act as a female to please him, and from his reactions she learns how to please males in general.[1] If she feels safe with her father, secure that he will not harm her in any way, then she can feel comfortable with her own sexual development.

43

When asked about early memories of their fathers, many fathers' daughters talk about "his smell," "his bigness," "his warmth," "his chest," "the thrill of being near his body." There is a visceral longing for the father's body, a desire to be held and to be loved. This longing for the father's body is the seed of a daughter's early sexual feelings.

One woman describes the size of her father's hands and how she loved it when he held her chin and brushed her hair. Another woman remembers sitting on the toilet seat at the age of three and watching her father, naked from the waist up, lather his face and shave. She was enthralled by the "glinty, golden hair on his body," and she swoons with the memory. Another woman recalls lying on her father's tummy as a baby, being rocked to sleep by the slow rhythm of his chest moving up and down. Another woman recounts climbing into bed between her parents, snuggling close to her father, and feeling a charge she would only describe in adulthood as sexual. Yet another recalls showering with her father and experiencing both curiosity and confusion in seeing his naked body.

Few daughters will admit that they had subconscious sexual feelings for their fathers in childhood; most are repulsed by the possibility. But many adult daughters recall the surprise of having sexual dreams about their fathers and waking up with conflicted feelings. Other women, like myself, experienced attraction to their fathers not in the literal sexual sense, but in the sense of feeling drawn strongly to their power or creativity. A daughter's childhood attraction to her father is both natural and healthy, particularly if the father does not violate the boundaries of a normal father-daughter relationship. He is her first love, and through his reciprocal love she knows she is desirable. The positive experience between daughter and father is the foundation for her future intimate relationships.

As a child, a father's daughter's yearning for her father typically excludes the mother, as we have seen. I remember my daughter Heather's exuberance during a walk with her dad on the beach when she was fourteen months old. One Sunday morning we took her and her older brother down to the sea so that Heather, who had been walking for two months, could learn how to navigate the sand. She was wearing a long print dress, vintage early seventies, covered with tiny red rosebuds and edged at the hem with lace. The red bow in her fine, black, curly hair blew in the ocean breeze. At first, she was tentative about this new ground under her feet. Her father ran a couple of steps ahead of her into the soft sand of a rising dune. He turned around, held out his arms to her, and called her name. She looked up into his face, squealed with delight, and without hesitation flew over the sand into his arms. They both giggled as he lifted her high into the air. In that moment, the deep love they shared was frozen in time. There was a communion between father and daughter that I, as wife and mother, would never share.

As I watched them, I remembered that same feeling of being loved, joyfully received, and held that I had felt only in my father's presence. I also recalled the vague knowledge that somehow my mother was being left out. I know that she was probably there, but as a child I had obliterated her from my awareness. In my mind, it was just *me* and *Daddy*. When we moved to our home in suburban New Jersey, I was three years old. In my memory we arrived at dusk and my father lifted me out of the backseat of an old green Packard. I was half asleep as he carried me up the front steps across the threshold. I felt safely cradled in his strong, muscular arms, and I was thrilled to be so close to him. I felt a bit like a princess being brought to a new castle, or like a bride coming home. My mother was only a shadow at the door.

The father helps his daughter differentiate herself from her mother; in the process, her identification with him plays a role in the evolution of her ability to love another. Part of her developmental task as she matures will be to resolve her early attachment to her father and transfer her love to another male.[2] The father must also be willing to let go of his daughter so that she is free to love another. According to Jungian analyst Andrew

Samuels, the father has a twofold task with his daughter: "The father's first fertilization helped to make the female baby. His second helps to bring forth the female adult, who is then free to drop her father when and if she needs to."[3]

A father's daughter must transform her father from the object of her idealization into a human being. This process typically begins during adolescence. If she fails to do this, she may continue to adore and depend upon him in adulthood, unconsciously binding her sexuality to him. Or she may find that the only way she can separate from him is through rejection. Either response will affect her ability to have an ongoing, healthy experience of her own sexuality.

Adolescence is a precarious time for girls. Most feel very insecure and awkward about the development of their breasts, the onset of menses, and all the other aspects of their sexual maturation. A father's daughter is particularly sensitive to how her father responds to the emergence of her sexuality. She wonders if he will still love her if she is no longer his little girl. She wants to be viewed as physically and sexually attractive to boys her age, but she doesn't want to lose her father's love.

A father's daughter is particularly sensitive to her father's remarks about her body, weight, and appearance. Negative feelings about her body that continue into adulthood are often seeded by a father's thoughtless teasing. On the other hand, a father's healthy admiration of his daughter will help her accept her emerging sexuality as normal and desirable. This will give her the confidence that she will be sexually attractive to a male when she is ready to enter into a relationship, and it will reassure her that she has her father's permission to do so.

Father as Safe Model

A father develops a close, healthy relationship with his daughter through his constancy, protection, clear communication, interest, and *appropriate affection*. She needs to feel safe with her father; she needs to know that he will not hurt her emotionally, physically, or sexually. A father who is comfortable with his own sexuality allows his daughter to grow up in an atmosphere in which sex is accepted as normal. She can then enjoy her sexuality as a healthy development and not as a threat to him. Such a father is a safe model who supports his daughter as she struggles with adolescence. He is interested in her relationships with boys, is willing to listen and give advice, but is not intrusive. He does not walk into her room unless invited, comment on the size of her breasts, or touch her inappropriately. Unlike a father who neutralizes his daughter's sexuality by phobically avoiding her physical changes and focusing only on her intellectual or athletic achievements, he notices her sexual development and affirms it.

Pat is a sixty-six-year-old physician who grew up in a household where everyone was comfortable with his or her own body. There was a very relaxed attitude about nudity in her family, and she never thought it unusual until she went away to boarding school and the girls dressed in the closet. She was at ease with her body and found others' embarrassment puzzling. Sex was never a taboo subject in her household; it was a non-issue.

"My father and I talked about everything," she says. "We didn't talk extensively about sex, but when the subject did come up, our conversation was comfortable. My father was warm, sensual, and as sexual as any man I have known, but he was never that way with me. Our relationship didn't have that aspect to it. There was nothing even vaguely sexual. Both of us are very sexual people, so I know I would have been aware of any undertone. The last time I sat on my father's lap I was twenty-four years old and wounded by an unfortunate love affair. He hugged me and said it would be okay."

Pat had a healthy relationship with both her father and mother, and her father did not rely on Pat to meet his emotional needs. These were met in his relationship with his wife, who was a suffragette and a strongly independent woman. This is often not the case for a father's daughter. As mentioned in chapter 1, such a daughter often becomes her father's idealized wife.

The Idealized Father and His Daughter's Sexuality

A father's daughter idealizes her father as the perfect male. By the time she is an adolescent she has internalized this image of masculine perfection, and by adulthood she has proceeded to project it onto the men she dates and evaluates for marriage. Of course, no man can fulfill this projected image because it is, indeed, an ideal.[4]

Because of the intensity of the father-daughter bond, a father's daughter often assumes the role of idealized wife to her father, particularly if the sexual or emotional relationship between her father and mother is impaired. A father's inability to have a healthy sexual relationship with his wife may be due to many factors: his psychosexual development, his relationship with his mother, his feelings about women, difficulties he has with his own sexuality, stresses incurred in his work life. Or his wife may have problems herself with sexuality and intimacy. If she rejects her husband, he may choose his daughter's company and attention. His daughter becomes his confidante; he tells her about his work, his troubled relationship with his wife, his concerns about the other children.

The daughter's favored position gives her a false sense of power, too much responsibility, and ultimately a deep sense of guilt. She is robbed of a normal childhood and adolescence when she becomes her father's intimate. These conversations have some value for the daughter in that she learns about the work world, male-female relationships, parenting, and how her father thinks. But the shared confidences also give her an inflated sense of importance and position that should be reserved for a wife.

Secrets, discussions, and even arguments between a father and daughter displace and diffuse the libidinal energy that is taboo in their relationship and provide a closeness that substitutes for sexual intimacy.

A client recalled, "I remember falling 'in love' with my father in a way that should have been reserved for a boyfriend. Nothing ever happened between us sexually, but I had sexual feelings for him and I'm repulsed by those memories. He's dead now, but he still has a hold on me."

A father's daughter feels guilty because of her favored position, but she doesn't know what to do about it. Hers is the marriage that wasn't supposed to be; she receives the treatment that should have been reserved for her mother. She becomes the "other woman." As a result, she is deprived of a close relationship with her mother and loses a nurturing female guide. Her mother is unable to support her daughter's emerging sexuality because it poses an additional, though unperceived threat to her position as wife.

Chelsea is an attractive woman in her early thirties with long chestnut hair. She has a successful career in publishing. When she was eight, her mother went back to school to get her master's degree and was gone a lot at night. Chelsea developed a very close relationship with her father, always sitting with him when he came home late for dinner and listening to the events of his day. She became his confidante. By the time she was thirteen, Chelsea began to realize that her parents were having a difficult time in their marriage, but her father never admitted there was a problem. He ignored it. Her mother was home less and less because of school, and then she began to teach.

"I became the wife," Chelsea reports. "My father started talking to me more maturely and expected me to act like an adult. But I wasn't mature; in fact, I was rebellious and acting out. It was a very confusing time for me because he treated me like a responsible adult but he was extremely uncomfortable with my

emerging sexuality. He never liked any of my boyfriends, and he didn't want me to like them either. He was openly critical of them and said that all they wanted to do was to rape his daughter.

"*I remember going into a furniture store with my father to buy a dresser for my room and the salesperson thought I was his wife (I looked older than thirteen). My father didn't bother to correct the salesperson. I felt dirty, shameful, and guilty, and these confused feelings continued throughout my adolescence. When I was sixteen he took me out to dinner for my birthday and ordered a bottle of wine for the two of us. It felt wonderful to be the recipient of all of his attention. No one could compare with him. It wasn't until I was twenty-one that I realized that the kind of attention he gave me was wrong and selfish. It felt like emotional incest. I became incredibly angry with him.*"

When Chelsea entered therapy, she asked her father to dinner to tell him that she felt their relationship during her adolescence had been inappropriate and that certain things about their present relationship made her uncomfortable. She thought that they could have a straightforward conversation, but he didn't understand what she was talking about. He was nostalgic for the good old days when she was his little girl, and she realized that he was not ready to give up his fantasies about her.

"*I'm engaged now to a man that my father likes,*" *she says.* "*He's on his best behavior with Jim. He sees that Jim loves me and that we are serious about each other, but he still doesn't see me for who I am, and I'm not hopeful that he ever will. I hope that when I get married and have a child, it will force him to see me as an adult in a way that he doesn't now. But I don't see him examining his fantasies about who I am, accepting who he is, and realizing how separate we really are.*"

When a father refuses to let his daughter grow beyond his fantasies of who she is, it makes it difficult for the two of them to have a mature relationship. The father's daughter still identifies with her father's values and who he wants her to be, and she's not so sure who she is herself. She will have to leave him, not only psychologically but perhaps geographically as well, to develop a sense of self. Chelsea moved more than three thousand miles away from her father to begin her separation process. She felt overshadowed by his desire to control her life, and she knew she needed to build a professional identity for herself as a first step toward feeling separate from him.

If a daughter has been deeply bonded to her father, she may displace her sexual energy onto a quest for achievement and success rather than transferring it to a love relationship. She is arrested emotionally and sexually at the age at which she assumed the role of her father's wife. It is unlikely, however, that she will acknowledge that their relationship has anything to do with her emotional or sexual immaturity. She may harbor a deep resentment toward her father, but she will deny the importance he still plays in her life. If he calls, however, she will come running.[5]

One of the difficulties a father's daughter encounters in developing intimacy is that every man will be a disappointment after her father; she will never be able to replicate the idealized relationship she had with him. She may be attracted to men like her father, but they will fail to live up to her expectations. Or she may pick a partner who is nothing like her father, hoping to avoid the comparison. Unconsciously or not, she feels that no man can adequately partner her after her father. Elizabeth, whom we met in chapter 2, says, "I idealized my father, and everyone knew that. I wasn't looking for a man who was *like* my father. I was looking for my *father*. Both of my husbands knew they would never live up to him, and when that became painfully evident, it was easy to get out of each marriage. I just called Daddy and he fixed things up." This may be an extreme example, but such a father enjoys the primary position in his daughter's life and has no real intention of relinquishing it.

Jungian analyst Linda Leonard describes how a daughter with an idealized father is bound to him in the same way a woman might be bound to an imaginary "ghostly lover." Such a daughter becomes fixated on her father and remains faithful to this "idealized husband," even when her father was predominantly absent.[6] After a couple of failed relationships, she may conclude that she will never find anyone like her father and so remains single or settles for a lover—man or woman—who cannot compete. In this way, she unconsciously reassures herself and her father that he will never be replaced.

Luella, the artist mentioned in chapter 2, married a man who was intellectually capable but did not have the dynamism, physical presence, athletic ability, or creative skills of her father. Her father disapproved of Luella's choice, but she knew that he wouldn't approve of anyone who wasn't a cookie-cutter image of himself.

"I remember my father saying, 'Seems like you're getting pretty serious about this guy.' When I said that I was, he replied, 'All I can say is, he's no world beater.' "

Luella knew that her father viewed her boyfriend as only average; he was not going to be a big achiever. She also knew that she was never going to find anyone like her father.

"For a long time my father was my Prince Charming," she says. "When I read Linda Leonard's book about the ghostly lover, I recognized that I was never going to find my father's match so I might as well not bother. That had been resolved for me. On some level he had already filled the bill magnificently, and nobody could measure up to that. Adam was less male and less demanding, and that is absolutely why I married him." They remained married for eleven years, and then Luella chose to love a woman.

In my clinical experience, I have found that the sexuality of many fathers' daughters remains unconsciously tied to their fathers throughout their adulthood. The father may react to his daughter's sexual development in many different ways—he may repress it, neutralize it through intellectualization, be jealous of it, or violate it. In each instance, he fails to provide the necessary support for the development of his daughter's healthy sexuality.

THE REPRESSIVE FATHER

Unlike the father who is a safe model, a father who is physically inhibited can have a destructive impact on his daughter's emerging sexuality through strict rules about her activities with boys, mocking remarks about her body, anger, and general uptightness.[7] His own sexuality repressed, he is terrified of his daughter exploring her sexual instincts. His fear leads to judgment about what he thinks is acceptable behavior for her. He may also be aware of, and perhaps appalled by, his feelings of attraction to her. He sublimates these feelings by being hostile toward her or by dominating her into submission by quoting chapter and verse from Scripture.

Sylvia is a very sexy woman of forty-five who looks fifteen years younger. She is a writer and single mother. She says, "My father was very attractive, but he was uncomfortable with his sexuality and saw sex as complicated, secret, and taboo. Sexual feelings were something I was not supposed to have; he was afraid of what I would do. His anger was repressive and paranoiac. I realized at thirteen that my father was angry because I was becoming sexual, but he didn't offer me any alternatives about what to do with my feelings. It was a very heated time between us. He would come out onto the street trying to catch me with my friends. When we saw him, we ran. Sneaking around behind his back was a way of making him mad. I realize now that we were actually involved in a sexual game of pursuit and repression."

Adolescence is a confusing time for the daughter of a repressive father. The father who has been loved and revered suddenly becomes a controlling jailer. His daughter feels his disapproval of her sexuality and learns to hide it or to rebel. As an adult, she may recoil from any display of emotional or sexual feelings, or she may challenge others to accept her sexual attractiveness.

THE INTELLECTUALIZING FATHER

The intellectualizing father is possessive of his daughter in a mental way, thus sidestepping the dangerous terrain of her physicality. In essence, he neutralizes her sexuality during her adolescence. He still wants a close relationship with her, so he ignores or rechannels any sexual feelings he might have. Unlike a repressive father who uses rules, religion, or hostility to control his daughter, the intellectualizing father appears to be a nice, involved guy who focuses considerable attention on his daughter's intellectual development, her athletic or artistic progress, or their mutual hobbies. Or he treats her like a son.

The daughter is aware that her father is uncomfortable with her emerging sexuality, and she unconsciously recognizes it as a threat to their relationship. She begins to view her sexual development as somewhat perilous and therefore denies her attraction to boys. She looks down on friends who are "boy crazy," avoids dating, and hides her developing body with baggy clothes. She is "above" all that.

Her father intensifies his focus on her mind during her adolescence by debating and arguing with her. The charge between them is mental or creative rather than sexual. Erotic feelings are sublimated by rational intercourse. She identifies with his intellectual or artistic prowess, thus avoiding taboo sexual feelings. To accept that she might have such feelings for her father would be a perversion, so she denies the emergence of *any* sexual feelings. The sexual development of such a father's daughter is arrested in adolescence, and she approaches all males from her intellect.

"The basis of my relationship with my father," says Marianne, *"was the exchange of ideas—what I call the 'erotic brain.'*

My sexuality was undermined by overintellectualization. My father would say, 'You're so smart, you can do anything.' He would also say, 'You look beautiful in that outfit and your hair looks great,' but the first message came through much louder." His implicit communication to her was that she looked fine, but it was far more important to him that she develop a great mind.

As a result, Marianne developed a pattern of neutralizing her sexuality and turning all the men she met into friends. "My dynamic with my father became part of my makeup," she says, "my design to neuter my own sexuality. Until my early thirties, I was terrified of sex, the male sex drive, and men's sexual power; in some ways my mental life was compensatory. I became very involved in Eastern religion, and there were periods during my twenties and thirties when I didn't care about sex at all."

In adulthood, Marianne developed a professional relationship with her boss that replicates the erotic intellectual relationship she had with her father. She is her boss's lover-mistress-confidante, although nothing physical has ever happened between them. Marianne remains chaste, but everyone at work is envious of her relationship with the boss, just as her mother and sister envied her relationship with her father.

THE JEALOUS FATHER

A jealous father may force his daughter to make a choice during adolescence that will affect her comfort with her own sexuality for the rest of her life. Such a father cannot tolerate the idea of losing his favorite daughter to another male, so he orders her to choose between them. In essence, he says, "Either you remain loyal to me or you choose your boyfriend. You can't have both. If you choose him, you lose my love." Either choice is impossible. His jealousy creates a double bind: If she remains loyal to her father, she can never sustain a satisfactory intimate relationship with another man; if she wants to experience her sexuality with another, she loses her father.

Barbara, a performance artist, grew up with a positive, easy-going father and a Scandinavian mother who was cold and remote. Her father was an active, powerful figure in the local business and political community, and Barbara adored him. The light of her life, he was fun to be with, in sharp contrast to her mother, who was always depressed.

Barbara was a typical "good girl" who did everything right. She got good grades in school and was a popular student leader. Her father rewarded her with his attention and approval and gave her everything she wanted. Their relationship was perfect until her late adolescence.

At that time, she fell in love with a boy who was older and clearly sexually appealing. Her father vehemently disapproved of him and told Barbara that she could no longer see him. It was the first time her father had ever said no to her, and she was stunned by his absolutism. They had always been able to talk through disagreements rationally, but on this subject her father was adamant. He was unmoved by her tears and told her that if she chose her boyfriend, Ed, he would have nothing more to do with her. She couldn't risk that. She says, "I was much closer to my father than my mother and I couldn't bear losing him. If I did, I would lose everything." She broke off the relationship with Ed.

Barbara went into a severe depression for a year and a half after this incident. In college she married a man her father approved of, but her father died shortly thereafter. She remained married for seventeen years but never really entered the marriage. She says she felt like a wanderer, "lost in a maze, split off from myself." She has triangulated her relationships with men ever since, choosing a lover with whom she can have an erotic relationship and, at the same time, a stable partner. She says, "I can't seem to break the duality and find a man who embodies both."

Like the mythical figure Persephone, abducted as a maiden into the underworld by Hades, Barbara's innocent view of the world was abducted by her father when he threatened to withdraw his love. Everything had been aglow in her life; she was the golden child. Then suddenly the world turned upside-down; it was no longer sunny and safe. She had trusted her father, and he had betrayed her. He was not the perfect, loving father he appeared to be; his love came at a price, payable in the currency of her total emotional and sexual allegiance. The choice he forced upon her branded her sexual feelings as dangerous and taboo.

When a father makes his daughter choose between her own sexuality and his love, her sexual feelings either are repressed or are acted out with men who, like Hades, are dark, dangerous, risk-taking outlaws. In both cases, the daughter's sexuality is separated from the rest of her life. The repression of her sexuality leaves her split internally, as this vital and unique energy remains inaccessible to her. The rebellious acting out of her sexuality results in her playing two roles; she is both the standard of propriety and the wild-woman seductress who retaliates against her father by choosing lovers of whom he would never approve.

Barbara wrote and dramatized the following poem to express what happened to her when her perfect father destroyed her idealization:

When I was young, I thought my father was perfect
He did everything right
Not only did he love me inordinately, he gave me unlimited access
and rewarded all my efforts to achieve,
teaching me like a boy and treating me like a girl.

> Come put your cheek next to mine,
> Cause the feeling most divine.

He was a funeral director
a euphemism for mortician.
He dealt with grieving and death.
He was a 'big-time' middle class operator.

> Come put your cheek next to mine,
> Cause the feeling most divine.

I rewarded all his dreams
Until I discovered love and sexuality.

Hysterical about my older, Catholic, uncouth, sexy boyfriend
My mother hit me in the face
They both sent me away to school
> Come put your check next to mine,
> Cause the feeling most divine.

Finally one fateful night this father I so adored said to me
"If you ever see Ed Martin again, you are not to consider yourself
my daughter."
I was crushed but inwardly seething
I felt as though I were put under a spell.
> Come put your cheek next to mine,
> Cause the feeling most divine.[8]

Barbara's father acted like a jealous lover, treating her like a wife. Barbara's mother was emotionally unavailable to her husband, so Barbara's father poured all of his love and attention into his daughter. His jealousy violated the boundaries of the parent-child relationship by assigning his daughter the role of wife and lover; in essence, it was psychological incest.[9] Although it does not cause the same scars as physical incest, psychological incest forges a very strong bond between parent and child, a deep mistrust of others, and a subversion of the child's developing self. For a long time, Barbara was unconscious of how her father's complete control over her decades earlier still prevented her from having a normal, healthy sex life in her adulthood. Like many fathers' daughters, she still struggles to meet her needs for both intimacy and autonomy in her relationships with men.

Like Luella, a father's daughter may find herself bound to a "ghostly lover," unable to find a mate who can compare with her father, or she may continually search for a powerful man to duplicate the emotional intensity she felt as her father's idealized wife. In contrast, she may reject the type of emotional dependency she shared with her father but then duplicate it in disguised form in her choice of spouse. For example, the daughter with a repressive father may choose a partner who appears to be comfortable with his own sexuality, only to discover that this comfort is a pretense concealing much sexual tension. The daughter of an intellectualizing father may choose a man with whom she can have a satisfying sexual relationship, only to find fault with his inability to stimulate her intellectually or creatively. The daughter of a jealous father may choose a lover who allows her individual freedom but never offers her security in his love. Perhaps one of the most repetitive problems is that of a father's daughter who equated the alliance she had with her father with closeness, and then in later years confuses the alliances she forges with other men with intimacy.[10] She knows little about true intimacy, however, or how to share her vulnerability with a peer, because her relationship with her father was not one of peers. Her father always had more power.

Giving His Daughter Away . . .
Or Not

When a father "gives his daughter away" in the wedding ceremony, the strength of the daughter-father bond and the need to sever it is ritualized for all to see. English professor Lynda Boose writes: "What the wedding ceremony is really all about is not the union of bride and groom (which comes during the wedding night) but the separation of daughter from father. From the structural dynamics of the ceremonial script, it seems clear that Western tradition has always recognized the peculiar force of the daughter-father bond and the need to invoke special powers to sever it."[11]

On an archetypal level, the groom's family and the bride's mother are irrelevant; the drama is occurring between father and daughter.[12] The father takes his virginal daughter by the hand and leads her up the aisle to the man awaiting her at the altar. He lifts her veil and kisses her face one last time. He then transfers her hand (and, presumably, her sexuality) to a younger, more virile man whose name she may choose to assume. The father returns from the altar alone to the congregation, and all eyes turn to the young couple.

The marriage of his daughter is his loss; he "pays" for his daughter's wedding. As Boose observes, "Having performed the loss of his daughter within a dialogue that masks loss under gift, having played out the structural drama of his own defeat, the father is required to return from the scene and from his seat in the congregation, watch his child discard his name and pledge henceforth to forsake all others—the 'others' that now include him."[13]

In taking the father's daughter in marriage, the groom receives another, more hidden gift from his father-in-law at the altar. If the daughter is unconscious of her attachment to her father, her husband now becomes the father of her childhood, and she becomes the child she once was. All of her unresolved feelings and issues regarding her father are projected onto her new husband. He receives her romantic fantasies, trust or lack thereof, competitiveness, greed, frozen sexuality, hostility, and desire to be protected and provided for. All of this is disguised in the small print of the marriage contract.

Many fathers refuse to view daughters as legitimate adults until they have walked them down the aisle. Such a father treats his unmarried daughter as a child, completely denying her sexuality and refusing to take her life seriously. At times she does the same. He discounts her choices and views her single status and childlessness as a dereliction of her duty as a woman.

Lauren says, "Because I'm not married, my father does not take my life seriously. He doesn't know how to relate to me. I think it's because I'm a full-grown, sexual woman, and he can't safely compartmentalize me. He doesn't know what I'm up to or whom I'm up to it with. He says, 'When are you going to stop this nonsense of living alone and either get married or come home?' He doesn't recognize that I have a life of my own."

Luella's father viewed her single life after her divorce with suspicion. Early one morning he barged into her house, unannounced, finding Luella with her female lover, confirming what he already knew intuitively.

"I was lying there in bed and heard these heavy footsteps on the stairs and thought, This is my father; he's heading up to the bedroom," Luella remembers. "At that moment the door blasted open and there he was. He said, 'I want to talk with you about your mother's car.' I didn't say, 'Get the hell out of here, you jerk.' I completely acquiesced. I was stunned. I covered up June's head with the sheet, put my robe on, and went downstairs."

Luella's father never acknowledged her sexual preference thereafter, but he did ask her if her lover took good care of the dogs. In her thirties, he still treated her like a child.

A woman who has chosen not to marry and have children may feel that she has failed her father. Even if she has given birth to her creative self, she may still feel a nagging sense of loss as a woman. In "Failing My Father, Finding Myself," author and editor Connie Zweig writes:

> My father dreamed of walking me down the aisle, slowly, grandly, to the hum of Mozart or Bach, in a black tux, satin-trimmed, with his upright athletic walk, his graying hair, his authoritative eye, and me in pearl-trimmed, cream-colored lace, radiant with hope, my arm resting on his lightly.
>
> My father dreamed of walking me down the aisle, slowly, grandly, until we reached an altar of flowers, high and full of the colors of spring. My father dreamed of the moment when he would lift my arm and place it on another, lightly, stepping back then to leave me, his daughter, standing in the next moment as a wife.[14]

Connie feels a secret sense of shame that no matter what she produces or creates, it will never be enough because she has failed to marry and give her father grandchildren.

> To my father, childlessness is a stain on my womanhood, a blemish on my worth, a failure of maturity. Adulthood for a woman means in some profound way to birth and care for young ones, helpless and dependent ones, so that to remain childless means to remain a child.[15]

She also knows, however, that her love for her father has kept her in some way bound to him. She realizes that her work in midlife as a single woman coming to terms with not having a child requires her separation from her father at the deepest levels. She writes:

> Today, my dad and I understand that we have been caught in a web of love, that the fibers which connect us have been too tightly wrapped. We have come to see that, even while living many miles apart, even while making very different choices, our love has shaped and molded our souls.
>
> And so we have tried to let each other go, giving up our illusions of each other, and letting other loves come first. We find it difficult to care deeply for each other in a way that does not bind. And so our relationship becomes like a spiritual practice: loving and letting go.
>
> As he has released me, I have been left to feel both a child's abandonment and an adult's relief. Now I turn toward male lovers with more freedom and more hope, no longer seeking my father's twin or my father's opposite, but simply a man who can give and receive love.[16]

Violating Boundaries

The father of a father's daughter may violate the psychological boundaries of the parent-child relationship quite unconsciously. This violation is sometimes difficult to discern because it looks as if the relationship is a very close and loving one. If the father solicits from his daughter the attention he should receive from his wife, however, he is failing to see his daughter as a *child* with separate needs of her own; he is putting her in an impossible position. Rejected by or in some way isolated from her mother as a result of the father's choice, she is a child craving attention who becomes her father's idealized wife. In the extreme, she becomes a pawn caught in the conflict that underlies the husband-wife relationship.

It is not within the scope of this book to explore the complicated issues involved in father-daughter incest. There are innumerable books that examine the subject in depth.[17] I would like to comment, however, on the enduring damage done to a father's daughter who is caught in a relationship that involves sexual abuse. Because her favored position with her father has resulted in her abandonment by her mother to one degree or another, she has come to rely solely on her father. If he violates her sexually, she has no one to turn to; she is completely abandoned. She will have difficulty trusting any man for the rest of her life. The first man she loved, her father, sought to control her sexually, and as a result she will fear male sexuality or abdicate herself to sexual misuse.

Gretchen is a successful screenwriter and producer in her early forties who has never had a successful long-term relationship. She ascribes her inability to find a man to whom she can make a commitment to her fear of being controlled. Her father's infatuation with her as a little girl turned into violation of her as an adolescent.

"I was absolutely my father's little girl. I could do nothing wrong; any word out of my mouth gave him great joy. When I got older, he started coming into my bedroom. I had this feeling that he owned me and his sentimental attachment to me gave him the right to invade me. He was a feeler—he was a breast man—and he said that it was his right to know how his daughter was developing."

Although she has enjoyed sexual relationships as an adult and likes being cared for, loved, and treated with affection, Gretchen remains terrified of being controlled by a man with whom she is having sex. She says, "Sexuality is a pervasive thing; if you are in a sexual relationship, being 'turned on' all the time becomes a very big distraction. I have the sense that I'd pay a big price for an ongoing intimate relationship because of this. The bottom line is control—I have to feel in control, and I never do once things get going. I know that my father's invasiveness has absolutely prevented me from having a long-term relationship with a man."

Being caught in an idealized father-daughter relationship that involves incest forges such a strong bond that it may take psychological dynamite to shatter the bond. A physical longing for a father can still occur in a woman long after she has dealt with the wounds of incest. The premature awakening of a daughter's sexuality by her father can cause feelings of arousal and yearning that later sexual relationships never satisfy. Thirty-eight-year-old Annie, who was repeatedly molested by her father as an adolescent, says that she has never been able to have an orgasm with her husband. She is afraid the excitation will unearth a flood of memories that she would rather leave buried.

Some of my clients initially make excuses for their fathers who have violated their boundaries; they cite rejecting mothers, economic difficulties, alcoholism, cultural permission, gender bias, or a desire for a father's love. Other women deny that any abuse occurred. Thirty-three-year-old Donna says, "It's too terrible to live side by side with 'Daddy's a good guy' and 'Daddy's a bad guy,' so you extinguish one of them." The split that occurs in a child's psyche causes her to lock away the unacceptable behavior in a compartment in her mind that is opened only later, when other aspects of her life become intolerable and she searches for the truth.

In some ways, it is much more difficult for a father's daughter to come to terms with psychological incest than with physical abuse. If there is no physical violation, she does not have clear indicators of her father's breach of her boundaries, and she may still be intensely connected to him. Being her father's favorite is too seductive to examine. Her lack of clear role differentiation may also cloud her ability to distinguish inappropriate emotional or sexual behavior of other men. In childhood, a father's daughter is so thrilled by her father's love and attention that it is very difficult for her, as an adult, to discern intrusive behavior.

Donkeyskin

"Donkeyskin" is a fairy tale recorded in the seventeenth century by the French writer and collector of fairy tales Charles Perrault. It captures the compelling sexual dynamic that can occur between a father's daughter and her father.

Once upon a time there was a king whose beautiful wife died leaving a daughter, Christabel, who closely resembled her mother in every way. The king was bereft at the loss of his wife and grieved for many years alone with his favorite donkey. When he looked upon his daughter in her adolescence, he fell madly in love with her, thinking that she was his dead wife. He vowed to wed her. She was aghast at his proclamation, but could think of no way to refuse his proposal without offending him. She went to consult her godmother, the Fairy of the Lilac Trees, to ask how to outwit her father. Her godmother told her that, when her father proposed marriage, she was to make the impossible request of asking for a dress the color of the sky.

Christabel did as she was told by her godmother; two days later she received a deep azure blue dress, the color of the sky. She again consulted her godmother for advice and was told to ask her father for a dress the color of the moon. Cristabel made her request and two days later she received a beautiful silver dress. Next she asked for a dress like the sun and again her request was granted. Finally, she asked for the skin of her father's favorite donkey, thinking that he would never kill the animal for her.

But the king wanted her so much that he gave the command to destroy his donkey. When the donkeyskin was given to her, the princess knew that there was nothing left for her to do but to flee the kingdom. She left concealed in the donkeyskin, taking with her the three dresses and a golden ring given to her by her godmother at their last meeting.

Christabel wandered in the countryside in distress until, finally, she came to live as a scullery maid at a farm where her father would never find her. She concealed her beauty by wearing the donkeyskin. Indeed, everyone called her "old Donkeyskin" and thought she was a true eccentric. One day a prince who lived in a far-off kingdom came to the home where she lived. He had been travelling and needed a place to rest for the night. The farmer's wife told Donkeyskin to bake him one of her delicious fruit cakes. She did as she was told, but was too shy to give it to the prince herself.

That night the prince happened to notice a light shining from underneath the door next to the kitchen. When he peeked through the keyhole, he saw Donkeyskin wearing one of her beautiful dresses, brushing her long golden hair. In the morning he asked about the beautiful maiden, but everyone laughed and said he must be dreaming. No beauty lived there, only old Donkeyskin who scoured the pots by day and kept company at night with bats. He returned to his kingdom and quickly fell ill with longing. No remedies cured him. He told his mother to send for one of Donkeyskin's cakes. The queen sent a messenger to Donkeyskin to ask her to make a cake for her ailing son. In her haste to cure the prince, she failed to notice that she dropped her golden ring in the batter as she baked the cake.

The prince ate the cake, discovered the ring, and his fever began to lift. He vowed that he would marry the woman whose finger fit the ring. The king, seeing his son's health improve, told his servants to search the kingdom for the woman. They searched the whole kingdom with no luck, until finally the prince asked if they had tried the ring on Donkeyskin's finger. Everyone laughed at the thought of trying the ring on the hand of a scullery maid, but the king was adamant and demanded that Donkeyskin be brought to the palace. Two royal courtiers went to the farm for Donkeyskin. She returned with them to the castle wearing her moon dress concealed underneath her donkeyskin.

The prince greeted Donkeyskin with kindness, but could not believe that she could be the woman he longed for. He slipped the ring on her finger and her donkeyskin fell to the floor, revealing a radiant princess in a silver dress. The prince immediately asked her to marry him and she accepted. All of the neighboring royalty were invited to the wedding, and when the princess's father arrived, he acknowledged his previous foolishness and wished her a long and happy life with the prince.[18]

Donkeyskin is a tale of psychological incest in which the father, out of his own desperate need, attempts to penetrate his daughter's innocence. Like Donkeyskin, a father's daughter is often unconscious of how deeply her relationship with her father violates her boundaries and how it can prevent her from having a healthy connection to her sexuality. Until the daughter is able to break the bond with her father—to flee his kingdom—she will not be able to have a successful intimate relationship with a lover. She will not be completely present for herself or her lover. Her body may respond in lovemaking, but she will not be free as long as her father still holds the key to her soul.[19]

PART II

Fathers' Daughters in the World

Daughters of Demeter by Joanne Battiste.
(Oil, 48 × 36 in., 1990.
Reprinted by permission of the artist.)

CHAPTER FOUR

Father as Hero/ Daughter as Destiny

The personal father inevitably embodies the archetype, which is what endows this figure with its fascinating power.
—C. G. Jung, *Freud and Psychoanalysis*

When I think about my father I have this incredible feeling. I realize he has his flaws, and he loses his temper, and sometimes he tries to make decisions for me, but he loves me so much and he's so warm, open, and supportive, I feel really lucky. I just wonder if I appreciate him enough.
—Tamar

THE child's experience of a parent is composed of the lived interactions between the child and the particular parent as well as the elements contained within the *archetype* of the parent. An archetype is an inborn pattern of images, ideas, and instinctual impulses that functions much like a hidden magnet; we cannot actually see such underlying patterns, but "we can see their images and we are propelled by their energy."[1] These archetypal images that come from the collective unconscious are the basic content of religions, mythologies, legends, and fairy tales.[2]

Jung writes, "The parental [archetype] is possessed of a quite extraordinary power; it influences the psychic life of the child so enormously that we must ask ourselves whether we may attribute such magical power to an ordinary human being at all."[3] Each child internalizes an image of her personal father that is influenced by the inherited image of the archetypal Father. The man who is the personal father automatically inherits qualities and functions of fathers who have existed for hundreds of thousands of years; he carries the "pattern" of Father. It is not essential that the man who is the actual father embody all of the attributes of the Father archetype; indeed, none do. Yet the archetypal influence is so strong that when a young daughter looks at her father, she sees not a mortal hampered by age, personality, limited abilities, or ill health but a magical, perfect figure shining with power and promise.

The promise to which the daughter clings most tenaciously is that her father will always protect her and provide for her. Father as archetype offers a sense of order, authority, protection, and power, both personally in the family and socially in the world. He represents the realm of thought, intellect, ideals, and values. The archetypal magnitude of the father automatically endows him with the status of hero. In his daughter's mind, he is larger than life and his deeds are exemplary. He is handsome, creative, judicious, generous, and powerful; he is a man among men. The father who has a good relationship with his wife reacts to his daughter's need for protection with appropriate boundaries; he does not need her emotional support to bolster the weak parts of his psyche. However, the father who has emotionally turned from his wife to his daughter, for whatever reason, uses his daughter's shining devotion to fill the holes in his life.

Just as the personal father embodies the archetype of Father for the daughter, the daughter embodies the archetype of Child for the father. Jung writes that the archetype of the Child "is a personification of vital forces quite outside the limited range of our conscious mind; of ways and possibilities of which our one-sided conscious mind knows nothing. . . . *It represents the strongest, most ineluctable urge in every being, namely the urge to realize itself.*"[4] [italics added]

A father's daughter embodies her father's potential future; she will make him whole. She will carry his youth, his whimsy, his intellect, his spirit, his unrealized dreams. She will continue his life. Because he is her hero, the father's daughter is the "chosen one" and unconsciously agrees to reflect whatever her father needs to have reflected. She either carries his projected wishes for her or emulates what she worships in him, whether he intends this for her or not. In my experience, I wanted to follow my father into his business but he never encouraged me to do so; this did not eliminate my desire to be like him. Two very powerful archetypes are activated in the father-daughter relationship—within the father, the feminine Child archetype (the pure, eternal, beautiful, virginal daughter) is activated through his daughter; and within the daughter, the Father archetype (embodying protection and masculine guidance) is activated through her father, thereby creating an endless desire to please and reflect him.

Father as Hero

Throughout countless cultures and mythologies, the hero is the individual (often, like Athena, Moses, or Jesus, marked by an unusual birth) who has battled past his personal, local, and historical limitations to reach a higher level of consciousness. The archetype of Hero represents the central unifying force in a community and serves as the axis of identification for each member. The twofold task of the Hero is to *withdraw* from the everyday life of the community, confront the mysteries of love and death, and then *return* to the community transformed into what Joseph Campbell calls the "Life Bringer," whose knowledge benefits and renews everyone. The community rejoices in his return.[5]

Since we no longer live in a tribal culture, we lack true community to receive and integrate the hero. Although we inherit the archetype, the spirit of the hero has undergone dramatic changes in the twentieth century. Jungian analyst June Singer writes that the hero has become "the individual who by strength or wit has prospered—often at the expense of less ambitious, weaker, or more socially conscious individuals. . . . The hero myth in modern culture expresses itself in the growth of great corporations, conceived and developed by dedicated individuals who let nothing stand in the way of their accomplishments."[6] Missing in today's heroic pattern is the triumphant return of the hero to the community in a *relational* capacity, in which he brings with him a spirit of cooperation and joint accomplishment rather than that of competition and dominance.

The archetype of Father as Hero incorporates both aspects of this century's version of the heroic pattern: The father enacts the first part of the heroic journey while abandoning the second. In the first part, the father is the bridge between the family and the outside world, and each day he is tested. Even with the dramatic changes that have occurred as a result of the women's movement and the high incidence of single-parent families headed by women, the patriarchal influence is still clearly dominant. The family identifies with the father's trials and triumphs and eagerly awaits his return. Like the hero in literature, the father-hero of the twentieth century *is* absent. Although it is his privilege to come and go as he pleases, this privilege carries an enormous burden. He is encouraged to abandon the home front in his task of serving society, yet he is expected to remain responsible for the welfare of his family.

Today's father is successful at slaying the dragon, but he has not been taught how to bring the boon home; the second part of the hero's journey has been collectively abandoned. As poet Robert Bly has stated, the child receives her father's temperament but not his teachings. The father is forced to carry an image (and its attendant glory) that may bear little resemblance to who he is as a person. Idealized as hero, particularly if he is absent, the father is invented by the child to be whatever she wishes him to be: more powerful, more knowing, more loving than any man could be. This response is exaggerated in the case of a father's daughter. In this situation, there can be little *true* relationship between father and daughter because the daughter idolizes the *image* she has created of her father and never gets to know the man. In addition, by virtue of her identification with him as hero, the father's daughter takes on aspects of the hero's journey by seeking to emulate her father's heroic tasks in the world while abandoning her feminine nature.[7]

Mythologizing the Father

Dr. Augustus Napier, coauthor of *The Family Crucible*, says, "Few of us, boys or girls, reach Father. In an effort to find out what he's like on the inside, we try to be like him. If I do what he does, act like he acts, perhaps I can know what he feels like."[8] We spend our whole lives trying to figure out who our father is. In our effort to know the man, we mythologize him, overlooking his most blatant flaws. In "Looking at My Father," poet Sharon Olds writes,

> I do not think I am deceived about him.
> I know about the drinking, I know he's a tease,
> obsessive, rigid, selfish, sentimental,
> but I could look at my father all day
> and not get enough . . .[9]

Olds writes for many of us, "I could look at my father all day and not get enough." But who are we really looking at? If I look into the face of my father, I can see my own potential waiting for me. If he is creative, I can be creative; if he is intelligent, I can be intelligent; if he is kind, I can be kind; if he is successful, then I can succeed. If he likes me, I can do anything. I am an extension of him. *But being an extension of him is not the same thing as getting to know him.*

We know our mothers better. We know their feelings, we watch their actions. We identify with their bodies. They are not the mystery that our fathers are, so they do not hold the intrigue, the fascination. We don't see our fathers cry; we rarely see them grieve or express fear. They are therefore seen as stronger than we are; implacable gods, they are in control of every situation. This control lies at the core of our hero worship.

A father's daughter views her father as a hero. If her relationship with her mother is negative, then *all* of her father's faults are overlooked and he becomes the "good parent." If the mother has been unable to nurture the daughter, the father becomes the daughter's lifeline. If the mother is rejected by the daughter, the father becomes her only love. In our archetypal rapture, we think our fathers are perfect, but our mothers do not. Sharon Olds writes,

> I even like to
> look in his mouth, stained brown with
> cigars and bourbon, my eyes sliding down the
> long amber roots of his teeth,
> right in there where Mother hated, and
> up the scorched satin of the sides and
> vault, even the knobs on the back of his
> tongue. I know he is not perfect but my
> body thinks his body is perfect,
> the fine stretched coarse pink
> skin, the big size of him, the
> sour-ball mass, darkness, hair,
> sex, legs even longer than mine,
> lovely feet.[10]

The daughter's idealized view of her father as hero imparts an aura of omnipotence with which she then identifies. In *The Other Side*, novelist Mary Gordon describes a scene in which an adolescent character, Darci, leaves a Howard Johnson's with her father, assured that she is his favorite child. Gordon writes: "She is the favorite. She is her father's favorite person in the world. Knowing this, she thinks she can do anything. She thinks to herself: As an old woman, I'll remember this, that I walked beside my father, I was seventeen, and I knew nothing was too much for me to do."[11]

This identification with the father as hero enables a father's daughter to feel that *all* things are possible for her. It gives her a distorted sense of her own worth and makes it very difficult for her to accept disappointments. After all, her father has assured her that she can succeed in anything she attempts to do, so a rejection from the outside world is devastating.

Twenty-five-year-old Jennifer always saw her father as a hero and, as an adult, has emulated him by following him into law. She says, "He's the all-American hero. He's generous, he served in the Vietnam War, he was a football quarterback, he's the all-American working guy. He stands up for people, he's not afraid to speak his mind, he knows who he is and likes being who he is. I feel fortunate that he's my dad. I think he's the greatest dad in the world, and I'm not the only one who thinks that. All my friends are overwhelmed every time they meet him and see how we get along, how nice he is, how funny. There's a sense of awe about how great a dad he is."

When Jennifer went in search of a job in the middle of her second year of law school, she couldn't understand why law firms were rejecting her. She said, "I knew that everyone else in my class was getting rejected, but I didn't see it that way. I thought, How could they reject me—I'm this person my dad said was so wonderful all these years. He said any law firm would be lucky to get me because I'm so charming, smart, and hard-working. How could a girl like this make it through law school and not be picked up by every firm in town?"

When a daughter continues to view her father as hero well into her adulthood, she refuses to accept that he is real and limited, not ideal and omnipotent. Her perception of him is frozen in time—most likely, it was frozen at some point during her early life. This dynamic makes it very difficult for her to accept the consequences of his aging.

Claire describes her father as having been, literally, the hero of their small community in West Virginia. He worked tirelessly as the town doctor, and everyone relied on him and loved him. He volunteered to serve in World War II even though his age exceeded the limit. He said that serving his country was his proudest moment.

Although both Claire and her brother experienced their father as "missing in action" from home during his wartime service, she did not—and does not—allow herself to dwell on the pain and loss his absence caused.[12] He was her hero then, and now, at fifty-two, she still reveres him as such, although his armor is beginning to lose some of its shine.

While Claire's father was busily occupied with the health care of the community, she was cared for by her father's brother, Uncle Ed, who functioned more as a father to her than her dad did. Ed is now dying, and Claire's eighty-four-year-old father is buckling under the inevitability of losing his brother. Claire says, "My father is not handling this loss well. Usually, he is the doctor, he is the strong one. But now he's acting really weird. My mother and I are taking care of this person who is usually taking care of everyone else, and that's hard. I don't know where he is, inside. I began to realize that he's not so strong now. I finally began to see that God is not godlike anymore."

Claire's inability to accept the normalcy of the grief and confusion of her father, a man now in his eighties, reflects the distortion of a father's daughter's hero worship. When a man is forced to carry the image of hero for his family, he is not allowed to have ordinary human failings like the rest of us. He has to maintain an ironclad facade, and when it begins to crumble, the family does not know what to do.

The Absent Hero

Like most fathers in the heroic pattern, Claire's father was away from home during much of her early childhood, but his absence was excused because he was doing his patriotic duty. The image of the father protecting the community is filled with power and righteousness. Although the child misses her father, when he is idealized as hero she justifies his absence. This is particularly true if he fulfills his archetypal function as protector and provider.

While Jennifer was in junior high and high school, her father worked long hours building his career as a litigator in a large law firm. Even when he was home, he had to work. She says, "He was home in body but not in mind. He would crash out early because he worked so hard. But he did it for us; I don't feel that he did it for his own selfishness."

As a child I, too, revered my father as hero, even though he was rarely home. He worked long hours in Manhattan, and because of his commute, he often returned home after my sister and I were in bed. I have few memories of spending time with him until I turned thirteen and began to work with him in his agency. My favorite memories from girlhood include the conversations we had driving back and forth from work during those hot, sticky high-school and college summers.

I was surprised to hear my father recently take responsibility for the toll his focus on work took on our family. "I guess I've never been satisfied," he said. "I drove myself, rationalizing that I did it for my family. One can always justify whatever one is doing to satisfy one's own ego. But it was an excuse; it was a bunch of bull. I got a lot of satisfaction from my work and I cheated your mother, your sister, and you along the way."

His admission stunned me. At one level I had always excused his absence as a child, thinking he had no choice *but* to work long hours. On another level, denied even to myself, I was furious that his work came before me. What was so important about advertising, anyway? His statement confirmed what I had not wanted to acknowledge all along: He had preferred his work life to his family. This truth allowed me to feel the anger I had buried all those years he was too busy to be with us, and then to feel my grief at the loss of his presence in my young life.

Adult daughters who excuse their fathers' absences overidentify with male achievement in the world. If a father won't join his daughter in her world, then she will join him in *his*. She does this by leaving her female world behind. She grows up quickly and abandons her feelings in order to be like her father, to win his attention, to carry forth his destiny.

Daughter as Destiny

The father who seeks to nurture and support his daughter's inherent talents does not project his destiny onto her. Instead, he observes her natural abilities and preferences and reinforces them. She does not activate the child archetype in him, because he is already engaged in living his own potential. He may be a hero to her for a while, but his relational alliance remains, appropriately, with his wife. Her hero worship of him therefore naturally dissipates during late adolescence and early adulthood.

In contrast, a father's daughter who embodies her father's unlived potential remains entrenched in hero worship and committed to long-term emulation of her father. At some point in adulthood, she will have to separate from her enmeshment with him, but in the meantime, entering his world can benefit her. Many women who gain admittance to their fathers' worlds through working with them develop the confidence that they, too, can participate and succeed. These early work experiences do not necessarily guarantee that career opportunities will be available to her in years to come, but she learns what is possible, and she is better equipped to pursue her options.[13]

The daughter's identification with her father as bridge to the outer world helps her find satisfaction in the world of work; *this is perhaps where her identification with him works most to her advantage.* The skills and abilities developed in the outer world eventually help some fathers' daughters individuate from their fathers to pursue their given talents and proclivities. They are then free to follow their own destinies. This was true for Tamar.

Tamar is a thirty-year-old New Yorker who has just opened an advertising agency. Her father has run his own engineering firm for the last twenty-three years. His father before him had a clothing manufacturing company named for his son. Tamar feels that she is continuing a family tradition by starting her own business.

"My inheritance from my father is to put myself on the line and reach for what I want. If it wasn't for my dad, I wouldn't have the self-confidence and courage to take this step. When I turned thirty, I decided to leave my job in publishing. I started to look for a job with an ad agency and my father said, 'Why join another agency? I think you can do it yourself.' I looked at him and said, 'What?' It was one of those ideas that you first resist, but with time it creeps in. After a week or two, we sat down and did a financial plan and talked the whole thing through. Little by little, it shaped up, and he's been there for me all along. He supported his belief in my capabilities by helping me do a serious financial forecast and giving me a loan for the first year of my business. One of the first things I

learned about being a woman was that women have equal intellectual capabilities, because my father just assumed I'd be able to keep up with him intellectually. Whatever insecurities I have, I never doubted that I would be smart enough to compete with anybody else."

In starting her business, Tamar chose to emulate the same values her father espoused in starting his business, as well as those of his father before him. She is proud to carry on this tradition and was encouraged to do so in the field of her choice. She learned about her father's world working for him during high school and college. It was there that she began to understand the intricacies of his profession, to see her father in a larger context as boss, and to envision herself working in a similarly independent setting. Tamar's father discussed his business with her then and still asks her opinion on decisions he makes for his firm now. His consideration of her ideas has helped her to feel like an equal. His acknowledgment of her mental skills has helped her gain enormous self-confidence. He not only supported her intelligence as a child but gave her, as an adult, the kind of support that says, "I believe in you, and I'm going to back you up." He assessed her skills and assured her that she was capable of meeting her goals. Tamar's difficulties as an adult have been in the area of relationships, not work. While her father did not project his unlived potential on her, he did form a strong alliance with her that has, to some degree, interfered with her ability to find a mate that can compare with him.

When a woman has the type of openhanded support from a father (or father surrogate) that Tamar had, she develops a very positive relationship to her inner masculine nature. She knows that she has the ability to succeed. She has developed what it takes to back herself up, and so she can move forward on her own steam. This is very different from a father who encourages his daughter out of his own need for her success.

Carrying a Father's Projection

A father who projects his needs for success on his daughter does not allow her to make independent choices. His ardent desire for her advancement is motivated by his need for her to actualize *his* unfulfilled dreams. He rarely sees her as a separate individual with desires and goals of her own. She is, instead, glistening with the archetypal potential she carries, unknowingly, for her father. Their relationship is so enmeshed and he monitors her life so intensely that the daughter does not realize she is suffocating under the weight of his control. In the following case, the daughter's devastation at her father's death signals the enormity of her enmeshment; her inability to function without him leads her, in desperation, to finally begin the inner work of disentangling herself from his projections.

Jacquie is a twenty-seven-year-old lawyer who started therapy eighteen months after her father died. She was out of work and immobilized by her grief. Devastated by her father's death, she felt lost without him. He had dominated her life, and she had never made a decision on her own. His death left her life in shambles, and she slowly began to face the shocking reality that her life had not been her own.

Jacquie and her father shared a very close relationship which she traces back to her first memory of his teaching her how to dance the polka, at age six. She proudly displays a photograph of him leading her through the intricate steps that won her many dance competitions. The ease with which she followed him on the dance floor made it natural for her to follow his directives in other areas. With equal enthusiasm he nurtured her intelligence and told her that she could accomplish anything. He was an immigrant from Yugoslavia and felt hampered by his accent, which he perceived as an impediment to his success in this country. In this area he could not lead the way for Jacquie, but he was fiercely determined that Jacquie would experience no such limitations herself.

Jacquie went to law school because of her father. He believed lawyers had the prestige, power, and money to succeed in this culture. As a young girl, Jacquie had hoped to work with children as a teacher or psychologist, but her father denigrated teaching as a "woman's" profession, felt that psychologists didn't make enough money, and told her she lacked the stamina to make it through medical school and become a psychiatrist. He dismissed psychology as worthless. He wanted a lawyer in the family, and Jacquie, as the youngest, was left to fulfill his dream. Jacquie's mother colluded with her husband and told her daughter to listen to him.

Jacquie hated law school. She wanted to leave during her first semester, but her father ignored her distress. He assumed that her love life was interfering with her studies and told her to buckle down and work. Miserable, she completed the three years and passed the bar. Ironically, he died before he saw her installed as a lawyer.

Stricken by his death, Jacquie was unable to find a job that would satisfy her needs as well as the needs of her father, which she had dutifully internalized. He wielded as much weight from the grave as he had in life. She wanted to go into the child-abuse field but knew that he would have disapproved. In therapy, she gradually realized she had to let him die in order to pursue her own dreams. She began to feel rage that he had lived vicariously through her, totally disregarding her needs, her dreams. In trying to give voice to feelings never uttered while he lived, she wrote her father a letter:

Dear Dad,
    You were my hero, do you know that? You were my first love, my ideal of the perfect man. I admired you and respected you and lived for you. I was your shadow, and we had a lot of fun together. But I never felt like I truly pleased you. No matter what I

did, it was never enough. I have tried my whole life to make you proud and now I am caught between pleasing you and satisfying myself. I would give anything to make you proud, just once. But I am paralyzed; I can do nothing.

Jacquie began to see how controlling and manipulative her father had been, molding *her life* to satisfy *his needs*. He repeatedly interfered with her relationships with men, criticizing her choices as never good enough. And although she was special, he felt she could always be better, do more. In therapy, Jacquie grieved the loss of her father as hero and raged at the man who had robbed her of her own dreams. Only then could she slowly learn to listen to her own feelings.

After several months of therapy, Jacquie got a job representing children who have been sexually abused and began a relationship with a man who is accepting and loving and who doesn't try to change her. She is also considering a return to graduate school to pursue a degree in child counseling. She knows that she inherited her feelings of inadequacy from her father's insecurities about his immigrant status. She also knows that he loved her and wanted her to be happy, but now she knows that she can be happy only by making her own choices and living her own life.

In the next case, it is the father who is devastated by separation from the daughter. This father's daughter, unlike most, was able to shed her father's projections in early adulthood. As a writer, she vividly describes the consuming need of her father to see himself reflected in her life.

In her autobiography, *The Bookmaker's Daughter*, Shirley Abbott writes: "If our lives had been a newsreel, my father would have been the narrator—the soothsayer, the bard, the scop. I was born, he thought, to listen, and I understood that listening was the essential votive act. Friends, Romans, countrymen, lend me your ears. Attention was what he needed, and I had the power to bestow it."[14]

Abbott grew up in the 1940s and 1950s in Arkansas, the only child of a father whose job was taking bets on horses and paying off the winnings. When he married her mother, he allowed his young wife to think that he made books of another kind. His great love was the printed word, and he shared this passion with his daughter. "My mother was determined that I should be like other girls, while my father was determined to make me different. He shared his passions with me, heaped my plate with them as if they were T-bone steaks and mashed potatoes. Romans (with Greeks lurking around the edges) were the roast prime rib *au jus* of history and literature."[15]

Abbott's father gloried in her love of their shared passion—a passion that fired the dreams he could only glimpse, in part, through his daughter. When she grew to adulthood and left the South to work in New York City, he became a broken man, a lowly bet-taker. In living out her dreams for herself, Abbott had to leave her father behind. She knew that he considered her a traitor, but she also knew that he himself had prepared her for her destiny. "I am my own creature, I said to myself. 'Daughter' is not a lifelong assignment."[16]

Daughter as Son

A daughter who carries the child archetype for her father finds that she may be given, and may unconsciously assume, the role of son. A father who has not sired a son, or whose son has been a disappointment, often turns to his daughter to reflect his dreams and be his heir. He relates to her as male, giving her certain responsibilities and privileges denied to other siblings; he implies to his daughter that he would prefer it if she were a boy; in that way she could carry his destiny in the way a son would. This father, consumed by his desire for continuation of his lineage (his dreams and potential), is different from the intellectualizing father (described in chapter 3), who neuters his daughter by focusing on her mental development as a defense against her emerging sexuality. Sexuality is not the focus here; destiny is. Therefore, this father encourages his daughter's abilities and talents as long as they mirror his own. It appears that he supports her autonomy, but in fact he does not. Such a father sees his daughter solely as a reflection of himself.

The father's daughter who is treated like a son is not reinforced for her femaleness but for her "masculine" traits and skills. She is usually a tomboy as a young girl. The father teaches her how to think, argue, and compete like a man. Having chosen her father over her mother, she grows up with lingering regrets about being a woman. She has learned from her father to feel superior in the male world, but at the same time she feels inadequate as a woman because she has not learned the ways of the "female world." She is in an impossible bind; she appears outwardly confident, but because this confidence is based on her inflation, she often feels like a fraud.

The father who directly or indirectly communicates to his daughter that it is preferable to be a boy robs her of the joys of being female. To fully accept herself as a woman in adulthood, this daughter has to demythologize her father as hero and disidentify herself as his son. The daughter as son must die for the adult woman to live.

When I began to write this section, I had the following dream about a father sacrificing his son:

I am sitting in a high school theater watching a film in which a son is sacrificed by his father, who is the king, in order to retain ownership of lands coveted by the father's brother. The king carries his son to a parapet and shows him the lands of the kingdom. "This is your kingdom," he says to the boy. They then watch together as the uncle gallops toward the castle and calls for the boy. The king tells his son that he must go forward and meet his uncle bravely. The boy instantly foresees his fate and embraces it. His loyalty to his father demands compliance; he has no choice but to go to his death to save the land. The film ends, and it is intermission.

I am seated in the back of the theater on the right-hand side. My father is seated in the front on the left. I want to introduce him to my favorite math teacher, but I cannot locate her. I also want to be seen with my father—we look alike—by some boy in the back whom I am trying to impress. When intermission ends, my father sits down and I return to my seat in the back. The film begins again, and the same scene is repeated. The father-king walks with his son to meet his uncle. The child knows that he is to be sacrificed for the land. He looks at his father and says, "Isn't there another way?" His father does not respond, and the child knows that his fate is sealed by his father's silence. He walks forward to meet his uncle's sword.

In this dream I am the boy child. The dream tells me *twice* what my fate is to be; it is my destiny to be sacrificed for the father. I grew up in a household in which my father was absent most of the time because of his commitment to work, and I always thought he would have stayed at home if he had had a son. My mother resented my father for abandoning her for his work, and she took out her frustration on me and my sister. As a child I did not deserve her anger, but it was my *fate* to receive the feelings that rightfully belonged to him.

Jungian analyst Gilda Frantz writes that when the father abandons the mother (through work, death, divorce, indifference, alcoholism, etc.), the mother unconsciously abandons the child. The mother, herself deprived of love and nurturance within the marital relationship, is not able to embody the maternal archetype; she cannot nurture her own child. Instead, she becomes the needy, devouring mother, manifesting the negative pole of the archetype.[17] In my dream, the child realizes just before he is to be sacrificed that there is no way out. The father's silence confirms the child's fate. The father does not respond to his son's plea; he has decided to sacrifice the child rather than lose his kingdom to his brother. The blood of a child is shed for the supremacy of the king, and no wisdom is gained.

As a young girl, I told my father about my mother's anger.

He listened but never took action. He stayed at work, she felt abandoned and enraged, and I remained unprotected. Just as the child in the dream was sacrificed for his father's kingdom, my mother, sister, and I were sacrificed for my father's ambition.

The Price of Heroism: The Sacrifice of the Feminine

Jungian analyst Marion Woodman writes, "While all women are not fathers' daughters, we are all daughters of the patriarchy, and although we are becoming more aware of oppression, *we need to open our eyes to the projection of our intelligence, strength and feelings onto men.*"[18] [italics added] Since the rise of contemporary feminism, women have struggled for equality in the male-dominated systems of politics, business, and economics. Nonetheless, many women remain unaware of how deeply they continue to identify with and reflect patriarchal values. A daughter internalizes societal messages about her gender as surely as she internalizes her parents' more specific messages in this area. These societal messages continue to support masculine prominence and domination in every echelon. Although contemporary woman's position in society carries more visibility and power than that of her mother, she is still far from equal.

Perhaps the dream tells us that our collective identification with the masculine—the son—has to die in order for the daughter to be born. The birth of the feminine will rise out of the blood of the son. Women's identification with patriarchal control must die in order for them to become conscious of their feminine nature. Women and the feminine values they embody have been sacrificed for the father for millennia, and the old myths that serve the patriarchy are deeply embedded in our collective consciousness. None is more poignant than the fate that befell the daughters of the Greek tragic hero Agamemnon. Both daughters gave their lives for the patriarchy, one in innocence and one in hatred—a theme re-enacted the world over, even today.

Agamemnon sacrificed one of his daughters, the innocent virgin Iphigenia, in order to gain the winds necessary to speed his fleet to Troy. His mission there was to rescue Helen, the wife of his brother, Menelaus, who had been abducted by the Trojan hero Paris. The Greek fleets were assembled at Aulis to make ready for the invasion of Troy, but a dead calm lay over the sea. They could not sail until Agamemnon sacrificed his young daughter to appease the goddess Artemis. Agamemnon deceived Iphigenia by summoning her to Aulis with the promise of marriage to the noble warrior Achilles.

Agamemnon's wife, Clytemnestra, was not able to prevent the death of her daughter, and her grief for her lost child turned into hatred for her husband. After his triumphant return to Greece from Troy, Clytemnestra killed him. Their eldest daughter, Electra, spent the rest of her life mourning the death of her father, living unwashed in rags outside the castle, waiting for her brother Orestes to avenge their father's death. Bound in hate, she lost the ability to recover her own life.

A father's daughter is a casualty of the patriarchy to the degree to which she has served patriarchal standards—the degree to which she has absorbed the rule and role of the father. In *The Ravaged Bridegroom*, Marion Woodman writes:

> A woman who has mirrored her father since infancy . . . has little, if any, feminine identity grounded in her own female body. Her concept of femininity is a man's notion of what is feminine, and her self-esteem is dependent on men's smiles of approval. She performs, whether from the soles of her delicate Guccis or her sturdy Oxfords. Professionally and socially, she automatically becomes the mirror in which men see their inner woman. In an intimate relationship, she sculpts herself to manifest her lover's image.[19]

The father in my dream says, "This is your kingdom, and you must die for it"—so it is a kingdom devoid of *relational* values. The father's kingdom does not value the child, the soul; it values order, law, property, logic, and hierarchy. The legacy of the sacrifice of the daughter must come to an end. It is very difficult to value feminine attributes in a family or culture that reveres the father—unless the daughter wakes up. A father's daughter who has never examined her father's shadow qualities—his selfishness, greed, rage, denial—exalts men and their values as exemplary. They are like gods. The mother has been discarded in disdain. For such a woman, to become conscious of her feminine nature feels like a betrayal of the father. She is accustomed to reflecting *his* nature, not her own. Her own feminine essence will remain dim until she starts to pay attention to her voice, her dreams, and her body.

When Nancy, whom we met in chapter 2, developed vaginal infections, she was forced to become conscious of her feminine nature—conscious that she had neglected it—in a very concrete way. At the age of thirty, she was at the pinnacle of her career, a successful attorney in a firm that handles "the biggest, most high-powered, sexiest, multimillion-dollar bankruptcy cases in the country." She called her firm the "macho of the macho." She had just finished working out-of-state for a year on a huge case; she had been the only woman on a team of lawyers that, in essence, became her family. When the year was over, the work-family disbanded, and she felt an enormous loss.

"When I came back from the East Coast, I knew I had been with the best of the best. This is what I had been working for. I was one of them. I finally had the family I had been striving to get through my job, but as soon as the project was over, they all just walked away. Now that my 'family' was gone, I thought to myself, if I ever have a family of my own, I certainly can't be the father! I'm going to have to be the mother of that family, and I'm not really acting like a woman. Then all the vaginal infec-

tions started. I wasn't conscious of what the infections meant at first; my body was just doing its thing. Then I finally realized that I didn't accept myself as a woman."

Realizing that all of her accomplishments had not made her happy, Nancy went into therapy to find out what she most wanted to do. As a child she had taken to heart the words of the theme song to The Man of La Mancha: "I shall impersonate a man, enter into my imagination and see him clearly." She had envisioned herself as a man who would go off to do battle. She did do battle, fearlessly, as an attorney, but realized that she was afraid to face what was inside her. "I really started to feel like there was a sunken chest way deep down inside me. I was afraid that if I opened it, I'd find toxic waste."

During the next year, Nancy healed her vaginal infections and eventually negotiated a five-month leave of absence from her firm so that she could pursue writing—something she had always yearned to do. Her colleagues did not understand what she was doing, engaged her in psychological warfare, belittled her desire to write, and wanted the "old Nancy" back. But Nancy did not want to return to her old ways; she wanted to reclaim herself as a woman. Finding her woman's voice has been a revelation.

"I have spent my adult life denigrating women's issues, thinking that, if they could really hold their own in a man's world, they would just do it. It's really interesting for me to admit that women have a voice of their own and rights of their own that are different from, but equally as valid as, men's."

The Death of the Hero and the Birth of the Heroine

At some point in her life, a father's daughter is faced with a heart-wrenching choice: either continue her hero worship of her father in order to preserve the intensity of their bond, or remove her father from his pedestal in order to live her own life. She cannot have it both ways. The film *The Music Box* is a vivid portrayal of a daughter who is forced to confront her idealization of her father and move beyond it in order to claim her own identity, separate from—even severed from—his. This film is a metaphor of the difficulty a daughter may have in separating herself from the enmeshment of the father-daughter bond. Fortunately, most fathers' daughters do not have to sever their relationships with their fathers in order to individuate from them, but they *do* have to look deeply into the nature of their relationships in order to free themselves from their projections.

In the opening scene of *The Music Box*, Annie Talbott, full of love and admiration, dances with her father, Mischa Lazlo. It is obvious that this widower, who took such tender yet strict care of Annie and her brother, is her hero. Annie is divorced, and Lazlo is a loving grandfather to her son, Mikey. She is oblivious to the fact that her father will shortly be accused of heinous war crimes committed during World War II. He is suspected of being the leader of a Special Section Aerocross death squad that executed Jews and Catholics in Hungary.

Horrified when her father is indicted, Annie is convinced that the indictment is a case of mistaken identity. She becomes his defense attorney and finds precedent for mistaken identity in a similar case. She successfully gains his acquittal, despite damaging evidence that erodes her confidence in his denial. Still, in the face of the prosecutor's probe about whether or not her father is a "beast," she cries, "He is *not* a monster. *I* am his daughter; I know him better than anyone."

Annie is forced to confront her delusions about her father only when she inadvertently discovers incontrovertibly damning photographs hidden in a music box that once belonged to her father's equally notorious buddy. The old photographs show Lazlo dressed in an S.S. Aerocross uniform, holding a gun to a victim's head. This evidence confirms accounts she had heard from survivors who testified in court. Horrified, Annie demands an explanation from her father. He denies the truth, telling her, "You're like a stranger. Mikey isn't going to believe you. Nobody is going to believe you. They're going to say you're crazy."

Annie knows then that her father will never admit the truth. His whole life has been a lie, and *she* has been his alibi. His role as dedicated family man conveniently belies his past as a cold-blooded murderer. Annie knew and loved the image that her father carefully projected, the image that he wanted her to continue to accept. Now that image is shattered, and she must accept who he truly is. This man who is her father is willing to sacrifice anyone, including her, to save himself.

Anguished, she severs the relationship completely. "I never want to see you again, Papa," she says. "I don't want Mikey to ever see you again. Papa, you're dead; you don't exist. Papa, you don't know how much I am going to miss you." Annie gives the incriminating photographs to the prosecutor.

In this compelling movie the daughter is shocked into seeing how her father used her for his own twisted purposes and how she had colluded in maintaining the facade he created. She risks becoming an outcast and destroying her family to unmask this fraudulent hero and reclaim her own moral autonomy, her own destiny. Severing her identification with the archetype of father as hero allows the emergence of a strong, individuated self.

The Music Box uses an extreme example to illustrate the powerful psychological truth that the father as hero must die (metaphorically) in order for the father's daughter to live her own life with integrity. Only when she separates the man from the archetype can she see and accept his darkness and limitations—as well as her own. Then she can go about the task of creating a life in her own image rather than living out the projection of his. For most fathers' daughters, the death of the father as hero does not come about as the result of one dramatic event. It is an accumulation of disillusionments about the father (or father substitutes) and disappointments in the daughter's own life. Ironically, this growing disenchantment prefaces the birth of the daughter's true self, even as this birth is accomplished through the "death" of the father as hero.

The Handless Maiden by Kristine McCallister.
(Graphite on acrylic ground on panel, 8 × 10 in., 1993.
Reprinted by permission of the artist.)

CHAPTER FIVE

Nurturing or Severing Creativity

Creativity cannot exist without the feminine principle, and I am sure God is not merely male or female but He-She—our Father-Mother God. All nature reflects this rhythmic and creative principle of feminism and femininity: the sea, the earth, the air, fire, and all life whether plant or animal. Even as they die, are born, grow, reproduce, and grow old in their cyclic time, so do we in lunar, solar, planetary cycles of meaning and change.

—Margaret Walker, "On Being Female, Black, and Free"

CREATIVITY is a birthright; each child is entitled to discover and express his or her innate creative potential. The creative process is a feminine process with cycles to be honored and respected like the cycles of nature. There are fertile periods of activity as well as times when ideas and images lie fallow. As a young girl becomes more conscious of her own desires and proclivities, she opens herself to fertilization by the creative impulse within; she may feel drawn to paint, dance, play the cello, become a gymnast, or sing opera. To realize her creative impulses she needs many moments of stimulation and challenge that call forth her talent, as well as the support of parents who allow her opportunities to experience success.

As we have seen, the father is viewed as the bridge from the inside world of protected merger with the mother to the outside world of independence and separate expression. The father often plays his first direct role in his daughter's development as the attractive outsider who lures her away from enmeshment with her mother toward a separate individuality.[1] In essence, the daughter is seduced by the appeal of her father's role; she wants to be special like him. She views her mother, in sharp contrast, as merely ordinary.

In *The Writer on Her Work*, Mary Gordon notes how she became a writer because her father, who viewed himself as the creative one in the family, wanted his daughter to be like him. Her mother was seen as ordinary because she worked at a clerical job to support the family.

> I had a charming father. In many crucial ways, he was innocent of sexism, although he may have substituted narcissism in its place. He wanted me to be like him. He was a writer, an unsuccessful writer, and my mother worked as a secretary to support us. Nevertheless he was a writer; he could think of himself as nothing else. He wanted me to be a writer too. I may have been born to be one, which made things easier. He died when I was seven. But even in those years we had together I learned well that I was *his* child, not my mother's. His mind was exalted, my mother's common. That she could earn the money to support us was only proof of the ordinariness of her nature, an ordinariness to which I was in no way heir. So I was taught to read at three, taught French at six, and taught to despise the world of women, the domestic. I was a docile child. I brought my father great joy, and I learned the pleasures of being a good girl.[2]

As an adult, Gordon came to realize that she had been as much her mother's daughter as her father's and that being her mother's daughter had greatly affected how she wrote.

> Had I been only my mother's daughter it is very possible that I would never have written: I may not have had the confidence required to embark upon a career so valueless in the eyes of the commonsense world. I did what my father wanted; I became a

writer. I grew used to giving him the credit. But now I see that I am the kind of writer I am because I am my mother's daughter. My father's tastes ran to the metaphysical. My mother taught me to listen to conversations at the dinner table; she taught me to remember jokes. My subject as a writer has far more to do with family happiness than with the music of the spheres.[3]

A daughter's relationship to her creativity is intimately influenced by her relationship with *both* her mother and her father, but her mother seldom receives the credit. Because the thinking function is associated with the masculine archetype, too often a woman's creativity is attributed to her connection with her father, while her mother's form of expression is ignored. Many a father feels that his daughter's soul is fertilized by *his* spirit, that *he* holds the keys that open the doorways of her mind. Jungian analyst Albert Kreinheder writes that a gifted woman's mind is first awakened by a father who tells her stories, asks her questions, and plays mental games with her:

My own daughter, as she grew up, became an avid reader with strong verbal facility. I believe this trend was partly fostered by a little game I played with her when she was two to five years of age. I would say words to her and have her repeat them after me, one after another—real jawbusters, as 'androgynous,' 'corporeal,' 'tintinnabulation,' etc. It was like planting spiritual seeds in her young mind of the highest developments of our culture—language and concepts.[4]

He goes on to compare his teaching of his daughter to the training of a movie dog: "This training reminds me of that given to the movie dog, Strongheart, who attentively sat on his haunches for fifteen to thirty minutes each day while his trainer read him passages of good literature. He was given the best that human beings had to offer; and he gave back the best of his world."[5] Unfortunately, many a father feels that teaching his daughter to repeat his thoughts and opinions is tantamount to being given the best that human beings have to offer. Helping a daughter learn how to think clearly is one thing; asking her to parrot one's thinking is another.

Recognized or not, the mother is still the primary nurturing parent in most families and the one who first helps her child develop language. It is she who is there to name things, describe their color, sound, and shape, and ask the child what she has learned. These early interactions between mother and child help the child become aware of the world around her. How the child is encouraged and supported to interact with that world *independently* becomes the key to her belief in her own creativity.

This belief in oneself as a creative person does not come easily for a father's daughter who, identified with her father, does not trust her own voice, her own ideas, her own images. She has become accustomed to her father's voice—to his ideas and perceptions—as the norm and fears that deviation from these will open her to criticism. Most of the women I interviewed for this book stated that their forays into the creative realm were tolerated but never seriously supported by their fathers. While not actually blocking their daughters' attempts at creative expression, this inattention or criticism had a dampening effect nonetheless. Some daughters were allowed to take dancing or art classes as "something that girls do," but when they asked to continue their studies seriously, they were actively discouraged, told that being a dancer was a short, painful career or that they would never be able to support themselves as an artist. Unlike the ideal father, whom we meet below, fathers of father's daughters can be quite conditional in the support they offer.

Father as Mentor

How a father responds to his daughter's ideas, dreams, and visions when she is young has an enormous impact on whether or not she will express her creative potential as an adult. In order for a child to take herself seriously, to value her own creative impulses, she needs to receive concrete support and encouragement from a parent or other significant adult. Her father's role in this area is central and crucial. A father validates his daughter's dreams and desires when he conveys an enthusiastic interest in her developing self-expression and a willingness to help her manifest her goals. Competing in a sport, practicing piano, becoming a painter, building a playhouse, and hiking the Appalachian Trail all require focus, energy, and specific skills. Ideally, a father who is a mentor for his daughter functions as a wise and loyal adviser, teacher, and nonjudgmental coach.

When a daughter feels seen and listened to by her father, she also feels *safe* in trying out different parts of herself, experimenting with her talents. She knows that someone is always there to back her up whether she succeeds or fails. This support gives her permission to be all that she is during a time in childhood when it is difficult to be different from her peers. If the father himself models the joys and demands of the creative life, she knows it is possible for her, too. All of these nurturing actions help the daughter develop a positive relationship to her own creative nature.

A father who is truly a mentor gives his daughter entree to the outside world, even if that world is beyond his grasp. He sees her as an equal, only temporarily in need of his protection. He helps her set goals, develop skills, and articulate her ideas, and *then he steps aside so that she can move beyond him.*

Flor is a thirty-six-year-old Latina psychotherapist. She is the older of two children who always identified more strongly with her father than her brother did. Her father taught her to be self-sufficient during her early years in revolution-torn Cuba and throughout the years of her adolescence in Los Angeles. She fondly recalls how, from her earliest memories, her father told her she could do anything she wanted to do. "Not only did he say that, he challenged me to do that. He entrusted me to do things by myself; he helped me become independent from him by teaching me to ride a bicycle so that I could go places by myself.

When Castro came to power, family members were separated and sent to different work camps. The first time I went to the children's work camp, at eleven, my father taught me how to build a hammock. A week before I was taken away from my family to go to the camp, he said, 'I don't know if you're going to be sleeping in a hammock, but I'm going to teach you how to make one just in case you have to know how.'

"When we got to the camp, they brought in a whole truck-load of burlap sacks, threw them on the ground, and said, 'This is to make hammocks.' Nobody knew how to do this except me, so I taught the other forty girls in my barrack how to make hammocks! I remember the other girls crying and feeling helpless, but I had the attitude that everything was going to be okay.

"When we came to the States and I learned how to drive a car, my father said, 'If you're going to drive a car, you have to know how to change a tire.' My mother was very protective and said, 'Don't do that, it's not a thing for girls.' But my father said, 'Sure, you can do it.' And he showed me how."

When it was time for Flor to go to college, her father, who had never gone to college himself and could not support her financially, supported her in every other way. "When I decided to change from medical school to psychology, he told me that whatever I wanted to do was okay. He would listen and sometimes say, 'This is what I think,' and he would suggest alternatives. But he never criticized my decisions. I think he feels the educational gap between us, but he has never let it be a gap. His courage in leaving Cuba gave me the courage to move away from my family to live in a new city. He sees in me the pioneer that he once was. When I told him I was thinking about moving to Seattle, he said, 'I wish I could move, but I'm too old. It's your life now; it's time for your vision.'"

Flor's father asked her what she wanted to do and gave her the emotional support to do it. He also knew when it was time to give her the space to move beyond him. He was a mentor in the best sense of the word, as was Michele's father.

Michele is a twenty-eight-year-old African-American who works as a deputy probation counselor with delinquent teenage girls. Her parents divorced when she was nine, and she was raised by her single father, who gave her an enormous sense of self-confidence. She says, "He taught me everything—how to drive, how to clean, even how to cook—when I wanted to learn. He encouraged me in positive ways; he told me I was bright and a good worker, so I felt that way about myself. He set limits I knew not to cross. He's a therapist, and although I don't think his profession influenced the field I've chosen, he is good with people and I am, too."

Michele's father modeled for her the importance of caring for people, and she now works with girls who have had no nurturing paternal influence in their lives. Both Flor and Michele have fathers with healthy egos who see their daughters as separate from themselves. They know the boundaries of the father-daughter relationship and do not project unmet needs onto their daughters. They point the way, lend support, and *step aside*. Each one, in his own way, supported his daughter as she set about actualizing her creative potential.

Many fathers of fathers' daughters are unable to act as supportive mentors when it comes to their daughters' creative expression because of the enmeshment, identification, and projection that so encompass their relationships. Such a father is so ego-identified with his daughter that he cannot recognize that she has talents or wishes of her own. The father may well model creative accomplishments yet dismiss his daughter's own creative efforts as unimportant or minimal. To create, one needs time, internal space, and *permission to fail*. If a father judges a daughter's first attempts harshly, she will fear experimentation and learn that it is not safe to make mistakes even as she continues to feel strongly drawn toward some type of creative expression. She will develop an inner critic who tells her that nothing she does has enough value but prods her to continue to try. On the other hand, a father may unconsciously attempt to experience his unrealized creative potential through his daughter, praising her to such an inflated degree that self-evaluation becomes impossible and her own dreams are lost in the fog of his delusions.

Father as Creative Model

A father who is a creative model inspires his daughter with his energy and skill even though he may fail to directly support her budding creativity. A father's daughter identifies with her father's creative power and assumes that she, too, has the *right to create*. (He is creative; therefore, so am I.) Even though her father may ignore her talent, she emulates his ability to express his own creative aspirations. In the following example, Samantha's father provided a passionate model of the creative life. However, because of his narcissistic absorption in his own artistic passion, the other members of his family were "in service" to the celebrity status of his work. His most important legacy to them was as a model of the creative life.

Samantha is a successful screenwriter who grew up with a father who was a famous music producer. Returning home from his studio at all hours of the day and night, he would play his latest recording at full volume. Whatever it was—Greek taverna music, jazz, rock 'n' roll—he was thrilled by the sound of the music he helped to create.

"He was enraptured by the music he made," Samantha says. "It gave him great joy. His opening line to us first thing in the morning would be, 'Listen to the chords Wes Montgomery is playing, listen to this bass line, can you hear what the cello is doing?' It was thrilling. He loved to educate us about what he was

hearing that was special to him. He helped us hear the way he heard, and he had the best ears in the business.''

In adolescence, when her friends were rebelling against their fathers, Samantha had a hard time rebelling against hers. As a teenager in the sixties, she found it difficult to distinguish herself from a father who had long hair and was recording Janis Joplin. To establish her own identity, in young adulthood she became an Ivy League–educated corporate attorney, graduating as one of the first women in a law school for men. Her father had been such a consuming presence in her life, she needed to carve out an identity separate from his, so her choice of law reflected more her need to differentiate herself from him than it did her true creative passion. Finally, after practicing law for fifteen years, she abandoned her career to become a writer, making a commitment to let it take her wherever it would. She attributes her courage in the face of the unknown consequences of this major life change to her father.

She says, "It gives me great joy to surrender to the creative process, which I learned from watching my father swoon with the beauty of the music he produced. That joy is such a special level of oneself to touch. Most people are lucky to feel it occasionally; I saw my father feel it a lot. And occasionally, I feel it, too. But the only reason I ever knew this kind of intense joy was possible was because I had seen it before. He gave me that.''

Samantha describes the spacious, fluid, expansive aspect of the creative process that becomes possible when one has permission to experiment. She watched her father work when the muse called him, and she learned about the highs and lows of the creative life. His ability to convey his love of sound gave her the courage to pursue her love of words. When she sold her first script and built her writing studio, her father's picture was the first thing she brought into her work space.

Whereas Samantha's father modeled the joys of the creative process, my father modeled the discipline and stamina needed to birth one's creative ideas. My father's critical eye and need for perfection dominated his creativity and shaped his responses to my early attempts to draw. His natural aptitude as an artist, as well as his high professional and personal standards, did not make him a patient teacher. The fact that, to his mind, I lacked innate ability diminished any skills I did have, as well as my desire to learn.

Still, my father always dreamed dreams, *big* dreams, and by his example he taught my sister and me that anything was possible if we put our minds to it. We were wide-eyed witnesses as he collected images and ideas in his travels and materialized these in each house he and my mother built. The marble foyer he laid in their present home duplicates a memory of an apartment house entry hall to which he delivered telegrams sixty years ago as a teenager in Manhattan.

Although my father did not directly support my artistic aspirations, he modeled the discipline and drive necessary to turn dreams into realities. He brought home an array of Prismacolor pencils and other art supplies that would satisfy any young girl's fantasies and gave me permission to try, but at the same time he placed me in a double bind: By modeling his talent he enticed me with possibilities, but his criticism informed me that *his* talent would never be mine. Nonetheless, I am grateful for his creative example, which inspired me to develop the discipline and my own will to write.

Father as Wounded Artist

Most men are interested in putting their stamp on the world in some indelible way, and many fathers try to extend their own achievements past their lifetimes by influencing or controlling what their children do with their lives.[6] Unfortunately, many men in this culture have had to forgo creative dreams because of the pressures of being male and the financial responsibilities associated with supporting a family. If they have forgotten the joy experienced in the process of creating or have had to compromise their own aesthetic, it is unlikely that they will be able to support their daughters' independent creative wills. In particular, if a father's creativity was unsupported or openly devalued in his youth, he may attempt to control and even "own" his daugther's creative expression.

Chelsea, whom we met in chapter 3, has always considered herself her father's daughter. "I look like my father, and I've always identified with him. He was lively, funny, and dramatic, and I was quite theatrical, too. My mother was clinically depressed and at times suicidal; needless to say, I didn't want to be anything like her. My father was generous, and I trusted his love."

Chelsea's father took a great interest in her education and creative talents. She wrote stories and plays at age eight, a novel by age eleven, and poetry from the time she was twelve. Her father read all of her work and loved everything she wrote. He was not artistic himself, although he played the trumpet. He had decided not to pursue music in a serious way, because he knew he would never be successful as a jazz musician and he was a highly competitive and success-oriented man.

Having abandoned his own creative potential, Chelsea's father turned his focus on her budding talents with such intensity that it took her years to distinguish where her true abilities began and his self-serving praise ended. By her late teens, she began to sense that his grandiose vision of her potential was hindering her development as a writer. He inflated her talent to such a degree that she couldn't distinguish her good writing from her bad.

"He wanted us to work together," she says. "He wanted me to write a Broadway musical with him. I began to realize his encouragement was more about him and his needs than it was about me. His expectations were always excessive, but I didn't

*want to disappoint him either. At that point, I still needed to
bask in his pride."*

When Chelsea decided to pursue a writing career in her early
twenties, she moved from the East Coast to Colorado and wrote
while working in a bookstore and as an artist's model. She knew
at the age of twenty-four that she had to separate from her father. *"He expected me to be both rich and an aspiring play-
wright at the same time. I was trying to construct a life-style as a
writer, and he was appalled by my lack of overnight success. He
lost respect for me; I had failed to actualize his dreams."*

Chelsea's father, like many fathers who entrust their daughters with their destiny, overidentified with her to such a degree
that he was unable to see her for herself. She knew she needed
distance from him; she had become so dependent on his view of
her that she had no view of herself that she could call her own.
His need for her success interfered with her need to write. She
wrote in Colorado for four years and then returned to the East
Coast and entered the world of publishing. She hasn't written
plays since, and she realizes that, in part, this inability is tied to
her internalization of her father's need for her to be successful.

Like Chelsea's father, Luella's father, whom we met in chapter 2, had artistic talent but never pursued a career as an artist.
However, he was always involved in creative projects and made
a successful living as a draftsman and builder. Luella grew up in
a Southern family where the American dream for a female child
was to compete in the Miss America contest. She was the oldest
of four children and got special treatment from her father because she had an aptitude for drawing. She copied a drawing of
his in first grade, which signaled the possibility that she carried
his talent.

*"As I got more and more involved in drawing, I think my fa-
ther saw me as emulating him, as inheriting his talent. He had an
aunt who was an artist, so he concluded I was the one who got
the 'family jewels.' He was always pleased that, as an adult, I*

was in the art business, that I exhibited my paintings, and that I was financially solvent."

Luella's father never allowed himself the time or space to reflect. He was driven by a deadline-oriented internal agenda, which Luella absorbed in the course of growing up with him. She still struggles with the incessant injunctions of her father's internalized voice. She tells the following story in an effort to trace the source of the breathless, relentless quality that has always surrounded her own creative endeavors:

"In 1976 my father took me and my husband on a trip around Scotland. We saw all of Scotland in a week, travelling at 190 miles per hour. It was absurd. My father was in a baroque form of himself; he was bent on showing us the scenes he had seen and telling us the history he knew. It was not about meandering or passing time. In fact, the way he took us on trips when I was a child was very much that way—manic. When he was in charge and behind the wheel, it was his deal and we were pretty much his hostages.

"Anyway, we stopped somewhere to ask directions from three little Scottish schoolgirls. They had braids and little lunch pails and were skipping along when we screeched to a halt. My father boomed, 'Which way to Dundee?'

"They all looked at each other and put their hands to their mouths, trying to figure out how to tell us which way to go. But they took too long for my father He yelled, 'Never mind!' and slammed down on the gas pedal. We went tearing off, kicking up gravel and leaving those three little girls looking at each other in bewilderment. They didn't even have a chance to speak—I could definitely identify with them! Many times growing up, I was left standing on the corner with the gravel kicked up in my face as my father sped off to his next destination."

Luella's father was always more concerned with schedules, goals, and staying active than he was with pausing, resting, or ruminating. Like many fathers' daughters, Luella contends with this internalized dynamic: being gripped by masculine energy *that focuses on schedules and completion instead of process and flow.*

"Although I had his implicit permission to be creative," she says, "I always had the impression that he encouraged me because I was a reflection of a talent he had never actualized in his own life. His double-binding message to me was 'Be an artist, but do it my way.' I didn't challenge his limits; it never occurred to me to test his love. I emulated his activity level and productiveness, but that didn't result in my creating art; I wound up feeling as if I were manufacturing art. The way I've worked in the past doesn't respect cycles, feminine values, and the rhythms of my body. I feel like I have to start over and find my own way before I'm too burnt out to try at all."

A father like Chelsea's sees his daughter as an extension of himself and inflates her talent, interfering with her ability to express her creativity freely. A father like Luella's is interested in his daughter's development only as it reflects his own talents. Both Chelsea and Luella have struggled to free themselves from their fathers' overidentification with their creative lives. Both women received their fathers' pressure to be creative but not their fathers' permission to create in a manner that was true to *themselves*. They needed the courage to defy their fathers' injunctions and a willingness to take a different path.

Unfortunately, many fathers' daughters sacrifice their creative power to the enmeshment of the father-daughter bond. A daughter who never claims her own creative self projects her creativity onto her father, who invites her to enter *his* world of images and fantasies. Her function is to link her father to his creative self, not to actualize her own. She is the *connector*, not the actor. She loses the ability to recognize her own creative responses and never fulfills her own aspirations. Like the miller in the tale of "The Handless Maiden" that follows, the father robs his daughter of her ability to create her own reality and trades it to the Devil for his own.

The Handless Maiden

In the Grimms' tale of sacrifice and loss between a father and his daughter, a miller who has fallen on hard times is tricked by a stranger in the woods to exchange "what stands behind his mill" for a treasure that will restore the miller's wealth.[7] The stranger says, "Why do you plague yourself with cutting wood? I will make you rich, if you will promise me what is standing behind your mill."[8] The miller agrees to this bargain, thinking that what stands behind his mill is an apple tree. The stranger says he will return in three years to collect his due. When the miller returns home from the woods, his wife scolds his foolishness. "That must have been the Devil!" she exclaims in horror. "He did not mean the apple tree, but our *daughter*, who was standing behind the mill sweeping the yard."[9]

The daughter has three years before the Devil can claim her, and during that time she lives a pious life. The day the Devil comes to fetch her, she bathes, dresses in white, and then draws a circle of chalk around herself. When the Devil sees the pail of water she used to wash herself, he cannot approach her and angrily says to the miller, "Take all water away from her, that she may no longer be able to wash herself, for otherwise I have no power over her."[10]

The miller complies in fear, and the next morning the Devil comes again to claim the daughter. This time she has wept on her hands, so once again he is unable to approach her. Furious, the Devil tells the miller to cut off his daughter's hands or he will take the miller himself.

The father is appalled by this request but nevertheless agrees to carry it out. In fear and shame he goes to his daughter and says: "My child, if I do not cut off both your hands, the Devil will carry me away, and in my terror I have promised to do it. Help me in my need, and forgive me the harm I do you." The daughter replies: "Dear father, do with me what you will, I am your child."[11]

111

The maiden lays down her hands on the chopping block, and her father severs them. The Devil comes again in the morning, but she has wept all night on the stumps and, once again, he cannot approach her. Having failed a third time, the Devil is obliged to relinquish all rights to the daughter.

The miller tells his daughter that because he has received great wealth as a result of her sacrifice, he will care for her well. She declines his offer, telling him that she can no longer stay with him. "Here I cannot stay, I will go forth, compassionate people will give me as much as I require."[12] She asks that her maimed hands be bound to her back, and she leaves. The tale continues as the maiden wanders into the world and meets a series of people who indeed help her learn to overcome further obstacles.

The Handless Maiden begins her separation from her father with the first stroke of the ax he wields. The innocent, unsuspecting daughter is sacrificed for her father, becoming conscious of the true nature of their relationship only after the sacrifice is endured. The miller in this story is "impoverished"; instead of doing the difficult but richly rewarding work of becoming conscious himself, he sacrifices his daughter, who symbolizes his feeling and creative functions. He severs his relationship to his inner feminine nature. The daughter gives up her hands, which represent her ability and power to create in the world. She is wounded in her creative function, but this wounding leads to her separation and individuation. No longer trusting that her father has her best interests at heart, for he is too wounded himself, she sees him for who he is: a parent willing to sacrifice his own offspring to save his life. This is a hard lesson for her to learn, but it is necessary if she is to be jolted out of her innocent state. She knows that now she must leave the house of the father to live her own life. She goes into the world with faith that she will receive the help she needs to create her way.

A father who has denied his own creative abilities in his quest for success and power will invariably ask the same sacrifice of his daughter. Like the foolish miller, he is unaware of his actions; his self-absorbed focus obstructs his view but not the harsh reality of his deed. The wounding of the daughter's creative power must be healed by the daughter herself, as the maiden knew when she departed. And although the maiden did not cry out when her father cut off her hands, most women do grieve the denial of their creativity. Healing must be sought in the blood of the wound; the daughter must no longer depend upon her father's approval to support her creative life.

The original wound of a father's daughter is the denial of her feminine self. The daughter's initial negation of her mother separates her from the creative realm of the Mothers she carries within herself. Cut off from the dark, moist, earthy, archetypal feminine, she is ultimately denied the mysteries of her creative power. A woman has to grow beyond the psychology of a father's daughter to mold and craft the reality she wishes to bring into form. Until she heals the deep wounding of her feminine nature, she will have no true power of her own.

King Lear Allotting His Kingdom to His Three Daughters
by Julia Margaret Cameron.
(Brown carbon autotype, 35.2 × 28.6 in., circa 1872.
Courtesy of The Royal Photographic Society, Bath.)

CHAPTER SIX

Women and Power

Behind the father stands the archetype of the father, and in
this pre-existent archetype lies the secret of the father's power,
just as the power which forces the bird to migrate is not produced by the bird itself but derives from its ancestors.
—Carl G. Jung, *Freud and Psychoanalysis*

FATHER as archetype has carried the power and privilege of
King, Protector, Priest, and even God in families and societies
for thousands of years. Law, order, and hierarchy are embodied
by the Father archetype, as is the promise of protection, suste-
nance, and identity. One positive manifestation of the Father archetype is the "wise king," around whom the kingdom (his
family) revolves. Like Solomon of the Old Testament, the wise
king uses his power fairly and with compassion and nurtures
those around him.[1]

In contrast, a negative manifestation of the Father archetype is
the "patriarchal king," who wields his power in rigid and unjust
ways. He presides over the kingdom (his family) in an autocratic
manner, eliciting fear and demanding complete obedience and
fealty. Like King Herod of the New Testament, the patriarchal
king is a tyrant, annihilating anyone who threatens his authority.

The personal father is endowed with the mysterious power and force of the Father archetype, and, like this archetype, he manifests both positive and negative qualities. A father who embodies the qualities of the wise king exercises his power in a judicious, productive, and generous manner, encouraging his daughter to use her abilities and compassion to effect positive change in the world. He empowers her to be all that she can be. He holds the respect and admiration of peers and family, and his daughter emulates his use of power in her personal life as well as in her community. She grows up with a strong sense of inner authority. Jackie Dupont-Walker is such a woman.

Dupont-Walker is a developer who has built a low-income apartment complex for senior citizens in Los Angeles. Her father used to take his five children out to vacant lots on the edge of Tallahassee, Florida, to talk to them about how the area could grow and develop. He was a minister who led bus boycotts and was the first African-American to run for office in his hometown since Reconstruction. Jackie emulated her father's vision and influence by affiliating the nonprofit community development corporation she heads with the local African Methodist Episcopal Church. She now uses her abilities as a developer to create affordable housing for the community.[2]

In contrast, the father who embodies the patriarchal king exercises his power in an authoritarian, even autocratic manner. He may be experienced as aloof, willful, narcissistic, cold, and demanding. Presiding over his wife and children, he sets the tone of the entire household. He cannot be approached directly by his children; his wife is the intermediary between the children and their father in matters of the heart and often in matters of the purse. The father defines the rules; the mother pleads for leniency, flexibility, and tolerance. In spite of the mother's access to her husband, the father still retains ultimate power. A daughter who grows up in such a household learns that power is hierarchical, fickle, and unjust and that she has no real authority of her own. She is taught, instead, that her worth must be earned and subordinated to the value of someone whose status is higher than hers.[3]

A current manual for Mormon boys quotes from a turn-of-the-century church leader and captures this type of patriarchal power:

> The patriarchal order is of divine origin and will continue throughout time and eternity. There is, then, a reason why men, women and children should understand this order and this authority in the households of the people of God. . . . It is not merely a question of who is perhaps best qualified. Neither is it wholly a question of who is living the most worthy life. It is a question largely of *law and order*.[4] [italics added]

Inherent in the archetype of the Father is the promise that he will use his power to protect and provide for his daughter. The way in which the personal father uses his power to fulfill this promise (whether he is a wise or patriarchal king) depends upon a variety of factors: the cultural, societal, and economic influences of the time as well as how he himself was fathered. In addition to these variables, and central to the promise made by the idealized father to his chosen daughter, is the father's exclusion of his wife in favor of the daughter. Under the unspoken terms of the covenant, the father, who is viewed by the daughter as perfect, strong, and loving, will use his power to take care of her as long as she remains loyal—*as long as she emulates the behaviors he values*—even when he is imperfect, self-involved, or absent.

The covenant takes different forms depending on the individual relationship between father and daughter. The daughter may unconsciously agree to never truly love another because her heart belongs to Daddy, or to take responsibility for her mother and siblings so that he is free to pursue his own adventures. She may unconsciously vow to never disappoint him and then spend her adult life exhausted with overachievements he never truly acknowledges, or she may cut off her feminine sensuality, creativity, and spirituality and agree to support only his. Only when the father's daughter recognizes the binding power of this unspoken covenant will she be able to redeem her own identity and reclaim the power she forfeited in the covenant.

A father's daughter does indeed have the "ear of the king"— she shares physical characteristics, talents, and points of view with her father that her mother and siblings do not share. She becomes her father's confidante and companion and, in this capacity, shares in some of his power. She has the illusion of being closest to the "throne," at least until adolescence, whereupon she may lose much of her father's attention as she develops an identity of her own. Even if her father fails to encourage her independent development, she will continue to serve his dictates, which she has faithfully internalized, well into adulthood. Although she may project these dictates onto another man or an institution, in effect she is still living by her father's rules. She will continue to define her identity, status, and value through the authority and power of the internalized father, whether this internalization is embodied by a spouse, a boss, a corporation, a teacher, an academic or religious institution, a political cause, or her actual father. The rules and opinions of her father, present or not, alive or dead, will define the geography of her inner world. Lydia, a nineteen-year-old college student, says, "I don't know what I would do without my father. I always consult him for advice, and he tells me to do whatever I want to do. But whatever he suggests is what I'll probably do. He is my prime motivator. I always try to make him proud. It would disappoint me not to be my best for him."

Many a woman is surprised to discover how tightly she is held by this desire to please her father and live according to his values, and how disempowered she may eventually feel as a result. One woman described how her father's rule, "Thou shalt not fail," kept her in a torturous marriage and prevented her from divorcing and admitting defeat. Because her father continued to occupy the "throne" of her psyche, she unconsciously diminished the wisdom of her self-authority and denied her need to leave the marriage until it negatively affected her health.

Such a father's daughter carries her father's voice as critic, judge, and censor and has trouble trusting herself.[5] Because most fathers' daughters have learned how to respond to and serve this internalized authority, they can participate with skill in the power dynamics of the masculine world; their most difficult challenge comes in developing a sense of inner authority that is as compelling as listening to Father.

Internal and External Power

There are many types of power—political, societal, creative, spiritual, and intellectual, to name just a few—and there are different ways to exercise power: through tactics that enforce domination, encourage cooperation, or facilitate inclusion. Our purpose here is to explore how a father's daughter internalizes an understanding of power in both its external and internal manifestations from her relationship with her father. External power is demonstrated through position, rank, and influence in any group, be it a family, a corporation, or a military, academic, political, or religious organization. People who wield external power have developed the ability to influence others. In the most positive circumstances, people in power inspire with their vision and convince others of the validity of their point of view with their passion. If they use their power to serve as wise stewards of those within their realm of influence, they usually command respect and elicit agreement in pursuing a particular path of action. So it is with the personal father. If a father's daughter has a father who exercises his power judiciously, she learns to use her power in the outer world wisely as well. If, on the other hand, her father exercises his power autocratically, she learns either to emulate or shun his self-important, rigid, and controlling behavior.

Internal power is a sense of inner authority or self-reliability. Children develop internal power by learning to make choices for themselves, based on their own feelings, and having those choices validated by their parents. They develop a sense of self-worth, confidence, and competence with the growing knowledge that they can make healthy decisions. The inner Self becomes their internal authority; they serve one god. This is in direct contrast to children who learn that they must respond in a particular way to the expectations and pressures of their parents (external authority) in order to assure their safety and security. The dictums of the parents, rather than the inner Self, rule these children. Although a father's daughter may internalize a positive expression of external power from her father, this is not always the case with internal power. As a father's daughter, she adopts the expectations and judgments of her father as her sole authority and struggles to acquire a deep sense of her own inner worth or self-empowerment. She doubts her internal authority and caves in with the first challenge, particularly from a male. Unable to discriminate what is true for her, she gives her power away to whomever she wishes to please.

Gender and Power

A sense of inner worth is necessary before a person can reach for a position of power. Many women I spoke with expressed reluctance to pursue power in the external world because of lack of know-how, lack of support, and gender prejudice within their families against females exercising power. Only a handful of women described how their fathers actively encouraged their aspirations and career goals or even expected them to achieve beyond mere subsistence level without a man. Pursuing external power entails risks, and most daughters are taught to play it safe. Signe Hammer puts it another way: "We haven't spent our lives competing with other girls and women in dominance hierarchies, learning the arts of cooperating, of giving and receiving favors, of working with girls and women whom we dislike. We've been relating to Daddy."[6]

Contemporary women are involved in an ongoing struggle to reconcile their pursuit of power and authority in the outer world with their desire for relationship. To pursue a path of power in today's world, a woman (or a man) risks separation and alienation; many women value interpersonal connection more than the single-minded, exclusionary energy needed to establish and maintain a position of power. And society tells them that this is what they are *supposed* to value. Harvard educator Carol Gilligan's groundbreaking developmental studies of girls and boys have shown that girls choose connection over competition, while boys choose the reverse.[7] This pattern, established in early childhood, continues into a woman's adult life with her family and career. In most family and work environments, women carry the focus of relatedness. Men in power often have the support of wives and children; they are cushioned and strengthened by the family environment. In contrast, many of the women who hold powerful positions in society today have had to choose among marriage, childbearing, childrearing, and pursuit of career.

Psychoanalyst Jean Baker Miller explains that women fear that if they pursue power in the world, they will be perceived as selfish and negligent of family. Women have grown up with the cultural and familial expectation that they will support the empowerment of others (bosses, husbands, sons), not themselves. They fear that if they become powerful themselves, they will be ostracized.[8]

Most women of my generation (and previous ones) grew up in families with mothers who did not have careers outside the home and therefore wielded no real power of any kind (political, financial, social, academic, or spiritual) in the outside world. Instead of identifying with their housebound mothers, these daughters began to identify with their fathers. Even if their fathers encouraged them to pursue careers in the male arena of work, there were few female role models to show them *how* to do so. As a consequence, their perception of the realms of *power* and *love* became clearly dichotomized: Daughters learned that they could not have both; they would be successful *either* in marriage and family life or in careers.

Times are changing. Women are gaining visibility and power in the outer world, and daughters of successive generations will not have to identify so exclusively with their fathers in order to envision themselves in successful careers as adults. From their mothers they will learn that work and love need not be mutually exclusive. Until then, however, daughters will continue to have conflicts about their role as women and their pursuit of power. Samantha, whom we met in chapter 5, talks about how such role confusion interfered with her development of clear career goals.

"On the one hand, I had a father who said, 'Whatever you want to do, you'll do well.' On the other, I had a mother who was very traditional and said, 'When you grow up, you'll get married, have children, and live in a nice house in the suburbs.' It was very confusing for me; I don't think I ever had actual career goals. Even though I chose a powerful profession, I remained oddly unfocused in an environment that was always clearly focused. I used to walk around the law firms that I worked in and see people working eighty hours a week to make partner, and I simply could not imagine it. That kind of drive was foreign to me. I don't think I had my own goals or a personal sense of drive until my early forties, when I started writing."

Jennifer, whom we met in chapter 4, had the opposite experience. Both parents, but especially her father, played a central role in cultivating her belief in her own abilities to succeed as a trial lawyer, a profession that archetypally epitomizes masculine uses of power. Jennifer remembers her father consistently encouraging her to do whatever she wanted to do. "He never said, 'That's not for girls' or 'Girls can't do that.' He taught me to take a point of view and to argue it. His motto was 'Stand by

what you believe in and defend it, no matter what.' I learned to
trust in and fight for what I wanted."

A child develops a set of goals and a belief in her ability to achieve these goals by assessing her skills and having her assessments affirmed. As discussed in chapter 2, a child learns to view herself as others see her. If a father perceives his daughter as intelligent, responsible, and potentially capable of exerting power and authority in the world, he will interact with her in ways that further support these qualities. Through his instruction and help in learning how to solve problems, master tasks, and take risks to reach goals, she will develop a strong sense of confidence and competency. Unfortunately, many fathers do not typically offer such concrete support to daughters, and fathers' daughters are no exception.

In *How to Father a Successful Daughter*, Nicky Marone cites studies that show that fathers emphasize problem solving and task mastery with sons, but with daughters they focus on a variety of benign behaviors such as joking, cajoling, encouraging, rescuing, protecting, and playing. Fathers set higher standards for boys and answer more task-oriented questions. With daughters, they are more concerned about their emotional comfort.[9] These divergent responses have two very different results: Sons acquire the expectation that they will solve problems and make high-level decisions as adults in positions of power; daughters, on the other hand, acquire the expectation that they will need protection, and their abilities to set goals and solve problems remain unexplored. The inference daughters draw from this lack of paternal support is that they have neither the right nor the ability to aspire to positions of power or authority in the world. Fathers' daughters find themselves in another bind: Because of their identification with their fathers, they acquire the expectation, like sons, that they can do anything, but they are not taught how. They are not taught specific skill mastery nor asked how they are going to achieve independent goals. They experience their fathers' enthusiasm about their potential, yet they feel ill equipped to satisfy their fathers' expectations.

I witnessed the gender descrepancy associated with goal setting one night at dinner with my father-in-law, his twenty-year-old son, Winthrop, my husband, and my nineteen-year-old daughter, Heather. The two men questioned Winthrop about his summer work plans. They discussed the possibilities of his working on a fishing boat in Alaska, on the campaign of a political associate in New York, or in a bank on Cape Cod. For twenty minutes they talked with him about the pros and cons of each possibility, about how he could achieve each goal, and the names of contacts they could offer him in each area. His desire to spend his junior year abroad studying in London was also explored.

They then turned to Heather and asked her about her summer plans. She said that she intended to spend the summer at home waitressing to save money for travel in Europe. They asked her what countries she wanted to visit, and that was the end of the discussion; there was no talk of alternatives, about the possibility of studying abroad, or about what she wanted to do after graduation. Instead, they teased her about her love life. Is waitressing any more mundane than fishing or clerking in a bank? Is travelling to Europe on your own less intriguing than getting there via a college study program? I don't think so. When I pointed out the differences in their communication with these two young adults, everyone was upset with me; the men for calling attention to their gender prejudice, and my daughter for the implication that the men had dismissed her. Although Heather does not consider herself, by definition, a father's daughter, the conversation is illustrative of the gender dynamics that typically occur between fathers and daughters. Old patterns die hard, particularly when we protect the father. It seems *everyone* colludes to deny the father's fallibility.

When a father fails to engage his daughter in supportive discussions about her goals and how she is going to achieve them, she does *not* get the message that she has power over her own destiny. Indeed, many women have been taught that their destiny is to wait to be rescued. One of the most telling findings of studies of parental behavior is that daughters are typically taught "learned helplessness." In a study conducted by researcher Jean Block in which parents were observed helping children solve a difficult puzzle, fathers picked up puzzle pieces and put them in place for their daughters *before* help was requested, but they waited patiently for their sons to find the solution. A daughter is not helped to function in the world by a father who insists on rescuing and fixing.

While these daughters were clearly taught "learned helplessness," fathers' daughters receive a more paradoxical message: They are taught to be assertive, like their fathers, yet when they do assert their independence, their fathers swoop in, take over, and patronize them. Statements such as "You'll always be my little girl" or "Here, I'll do it for you" ensure the daughter's sense of inadequacy and dependence. These behaviors only indulge the father's need to experience himself as hero while crippling the daughter's abilities to function as an individual. A daughter needs to know from her father that *she* is capable of handling any situation that arises, that he trusts her judgment, and that he will be there to support her with information and advice *if* she requests it.[10]

Gloria, an honors student in the ninth grade, wanted to build a three-dimensional model of a Shakespearean theater to use for her English project, an analysis of *The Merchant of Venice*. She collected the materials she needed, completed her design, and had started to score the cardboard for the model when her architect father returned home from work. "Gloria, that's a great idea, honey, but you're not designing it to scale. Here, let me show you how to do it."

Gloria, who loved and admired her father, moved to the side of the table. Three hours later, her father had completed the model of the theater. It was perfectly designed to scale, yet it made her feel miserable. It was too perfect. She knew her teacher would never believe she had built it, and her father had destroyed her delight in discovering her own design abilities. His "help" conveyed his belief that she could not construct the model alone. Gloria couldn't tell her father how she felt because she didn't want to hurt his feelings. She pretended that she loved the model of the theater, and then she went to her room and cried.

A young daughter whose father conveys to her that she cannot manage her life without him becomes panicked at the prospect of being independent. She feels powerless in her own right; her identity is tied to his. She frequently refers to her father in conversation, identifying with his status and power. In adulthood, she attaches herself to a powerful spouse or boss, lacking confidence in her ability to survive on her own.

Women Who Work for Their Fathers

Gender prejudices in parenting behaviors are also reflected in adulthood. Daughters who work for their fathers in business often have a difficult time persuading their fathers to take them seriously when it is time to succeed them in the position of boss and owner. Many fathers are uncomfortable having daughters at the helm of their businesses, and many daughters are discouraged from entering their fathers' businesses early in childhood, while sons are not only encouraged but often pressured. Most fathers will consider sons but not daughters as their heirs.

Journalist Barbara Marsh has examined the experiences of women who have attempted to succeed their fathers in their businesses; she reports that these women's efforts to move up the ladder of the family-business hierarchy often violated the unspoken family dictums that *only sons* would be considered. Although she found that women make exceptional family-business managers because they are cooperative and skilled at balancing family and business issues; they are consistently bypassed in favor of sons. She writes: "Studies show that daughters are expected to be—and, indeed, often are—nurturing, loyal, and undemanding, while sons are generally confrontational. Those daughters who ask for more [power in the family business] frequently get hurt."[11]

Interviewing daughters who worked for their fathers, Marsh found that many of these men refused to give daughters management authority until a crisis affected their own or their sons' capabilities. Mary McMahon, administrative vice-president at Petroleum International in Tulsa, Oklahoma, found that when she first worked for her father, he didn't take her seriously and wondered only when she was going to get married. Her brother was named his successor, and Mary, discouraged, left the company. She moved away with her new husband.

When Mary's brother died suddenly of a heart attack, her cancer-stricken father sought her assistance, acknowledging her business capabilities for the first time in her life. She became the company's top operating executive after her father's death and formed a family board of directors headed by her mother. She says, "It's working great. Everybody is getting along. None of this would ever have happened with my dad."[12]

Some fathers who run their own businesses do not give their daughters the same nuts-and-bolts information that they give their sons. The daughters are then told they do not have enough training. Marsh tells the story of Stacey, a teenage girl who had to fight to get the same training as her brothers in her father's construction company.

"Roger Johnsen, who runs a Rapid City, S.D., concrete contractor, gave his sons construction jobs when they were each sixteen, but he insisted that his teenage daughter start in the office. The daughter, Stacey, who loves competing with her brothers in sports and academics, fumed all summer. 'I hated it,' she says. 'I felt I was getting the raw end of the deal.' " The following summer she enlisted her mother's help to persuade her father to take her seriously. After she threatened to work for his competitor, her father finally allowed her to do construction work; by the end of the summer, they both agreed she had done an excellent job. She now can envision the possibility of helping to run the company some day.[13]

While I have no way of knowing whether the women in Marsh's study were actually fathers' daughters, it is likely that some were. I work with a father's daughter who had a similar experience. Carol is an only child and was put on a pedestal by her father. She worked summers with him in his hardware and lumber company in the Northwest and joined him full-time after college. She assumed that when her father retired, she would succeed him as owner and boss. After working in the business for eight years and managing it on weekends, she was stunned when her father bypassed her for a male manager. She felt betrayed. By employing her and then disempowering her in this way, her father conveyed two very conflicting messages: You are competent because you are my daughter, but your power is limited because you are a girl. These mixed messages paralyzed Carol, undermined her confidence in her abilities, and ultimately destroyed her dreams of succeeding her father.

Mothers versus Fathers as Models

Daughters will benefit when either parent ignores gender stereotypes to support their expression of self-empowerment. In *The Managerial Woman*, Margaret Hennig and Anne Jardim studied how a group of twenty-five extremely successful female corporate presidents and vice-presidents were influenced and supported by their fathers in their careers. They found that these women were usually firstborn daughters or only children of professional fathers. Their mothers were quiet women who deferred to their husbands. The authors' composite profile of the managerial woman depicted a father's daughter: She had had a special relationship with her father and was often treated the way a son would be treated.[14] Identifying with her father, the managerial woman typically pursued a career seriously until her middle to late thirties, when she then experienced a "delayed adolescence" in which more feminine interests such as creating a home and having a family became dominant. Having first achieved prominence in her field as well as acceptance from her male peers, she was able to "take a break" from her career. After this break, she reported a more emotionally and sexually satisfying life and, for the first time, saw herself as capable of moving toward the highest managerial levels in her firm. As fathers' daughters, these women first identified with their fathers, implicitly rejecting their mothers as role models, and then, only in mid-adulthood, reexamined the aspects of their feminine nature they had ignored in their pursuit of power.[15] Such a father's daughter typically prefers to run a corporation rather than a household and views the feminine as disempowered; she therefore devalues being a mother.

In contrast, daughters who have mothers who are strong, assertive role models learn more about the skills necessary to balance relationship and power in the world. This is one of the gifts lost to a father's daughter. A recent study by Dorothy W. Cantor and Toni Bernay of twenty-five women in elected office cites the beneficial influence of the mothers of these women in positions of power. The congresswomen, mayors, and governors in their study viewed their mothers and grandmothers as competent, influential people, despite the fact that most did not work outside the home. These mothers were seen as having as much power as their husbands in the domain of the home and were deeply involved in community service. They gave their daughters the message that it is okay to be both nurturing *and* aggressive as women. They also gave them permission to succeed in fields to which they themselves never had access.[16]

Pat, whom we met in chapter 3, is the chief medical consultant for the Division of Licensing and Certification in California's Department of Health Services. Pat was fortunate to have a strong, positive relationship with both of her parents. She has had a successful medical career for more than forty years, practicing as an anesthesiologist, teaching in university hospitals, setting up a family health center on a Navaho reservation, and working with state government officials to change health-care policy. Her mother was a feminist who worked as a volunteer for Planned Parenthood in the 1930s, during an era when it was illegal even to give contraceptive advice. Her message to Pat was loud and clear: "Women need to have careers. Of course, you're going to be something; you won't be just a girl and a mother." Pat's mother was several generations ahead of her time, and her father, an automobile dealer who was very comfortable with his wife's success, supported her ideas. He always told Pat, "Everybody should do what they want and believe they can succeed in." Because of both her parents' positive influence, Pat felt at ease to pursue positions of influence and power.

Competing with a Powerful Father

Power is a complex issue. Many women have avoided pursuing positions of power because of the way men have abused it. Women say that they do not want to perpetuate the male model of power that relies on dominance and hierarchy and requires separation and division among people. Nonetheless, many fathers' daughters with powerful fathers do seek to emulate them by achieving hierarchical power in their own right; they accept the use of position and power as both positive and necessary to effect change and achieve goals. To them, *power* is not a dirty word. Other fathers' daughters who have had powerful fathers reject all forms of power for very personal reasons. They experienced the consequences of having fathers who chose power over relationships, and they don't want to make the same choice. Such a daughter is in touch with her father's sacrifice of her, her mother, and her siblings. Even if the father's work is admired as heroic, the loss of time with her father keenly affects the favorite daughter, who feels like the sacrificial lamb.

Brenda is a forty-one-year-old writer whose father was the chief administrator of an environmental protection agency in the federal government. He had fifty-five-thousand employees working for him, and he was always available to "his people." According to Brenda, he cared more deeply for his employees and his task of saving wilderness areas than any administrator who preceded him. He ran his agency like a family, but he treated his family like a way station.

"The collective family of his agency was fine," says Brenda, "but the personal family was another matter entirely. We were in service to his job; our personal needs and desires were sacrificed for his professional climb. We became his emotional pit stop. He travelled throughout the country three weeks out of each month and then came home to us to refuel. He had no relationship with my mother, who suffered from manic-depression, so I was his wife and fueled him with emotional support."

Brenda grew up in the forest, her father's work environment, until the age of four. "Everything was very tactile. I crawled through the forest and around the cabin. There were no other children to play with, so I bonded with the animals. My father was very much a forest person, and he raised my younger sisters and me like tamed wild animals." However, when Brenda was eight, her father received a fellowship to Harvard to study administration, and everything changed when they moved to the city. The family was no longer part of nature (the feminine); instead, the father was learning how to manage and control nature.

"I respect my father's career of preservation. He was an incredibly gifted administrator, able to negotiate between the extremist environmental groups and federal agencies. But when all the luminaries of the federal government were giving speeches about him at his retirement party, two of us 'children' walked out. He had been both our mother and our father, and when he got on the fast track for power, we lost both. He lost us, as well as the deep sense of relationship to the natural world, to a bureaucratic, hierarchical world that was utterly ruthless as far as his children were concerned. We moved across the country every *other year so that he could experience every type of ecology. I went to sixteen different schools!*

"As much as I love my father and respect his work, I am very aware of his inflated ego. He's a lonely man who has no peers and is totally cut off from his feelings. When he left the forest, he abandoned not only his children but the gentle, sensitive side of himself as well. He had a deep sense of spirit living in the forest; after he lost his connection to nature, he lost his connection to himself."

After college, Brenda became an environmental writer and editor in order to balance her father's point of view. "I wasn't an adversary," she says. "I was the person left behind in the forest; I became the voice of the forest. He had so much power over the fate of the wilderness that I felt it was my job to be his conscience. In a strange, unconscious way, we struck a deal. He sought power and management and I carried spirit for him. Once he even asked me to write a vision statement for his agency.

"I love what he loves, but I don't love the way he loves it. He manages *nature*. His approach to nature is one of administration and control. He favors the managed use of forests for logging and recreation as well as the preservation of plant and animal diversity. He sees mankind as the wise guardians of the land that is ours. I don't see it that way. Land is not ours—it is beyond us. It is mysterious; it cannot be managed; and any attempt to relate to it in that kind of male-female way—where the land is the wife and the husband controls her—feels wrong to me.

"When he was chief, I felt that I had to go into high gear and write for the environmental groups that were his adversaries. Instead, I became a moderate, navigating between his federal world and the world of the extremist environmental groups. I found they shared the same fundamental characteristics; they both had a warrior mentality. I chose not to be in that war. In my writing I try to balance the two extremes."

After her father's retirement, Brenda was free to write about nature in her own style. "The minute he retired, I was able to take risks and claim my particular power. I left the environmen-

tal field and took my nature writing to a mystical place, using personal storytelling instead of political writing. He had a fit— he didn't approve of the fact that I was using my corporate pension to support my writing. Nevertheless, I had a tremendous burst of creativity and I wrote three books during that period."

Once Brenda retired from her "job" of serving as judge and sentry over her father's use of power, she was free to focus on herself and finally do the work that truly fuels her soul. She carries the forest in her heart, and her writing reflects this innermost commitment to nature. She is no longer in competition with her father, nor does she have to balance his political influence.

In therapy Brenda has discovered that, based on her experiences with her father, her rejection of all power as bad has crippled her sense of personal empowerment. "I was so afraid of becoming inflated like him, I wound up deflated instead. I still have a hard time owning my power. My fear is that, if I move into a position of power and influence like my father did, I will lose all hope of intimate relationship. Standing up in front of people to do readings from my books was very difficult at first, but over the years I've learned to enjoy it, as long as I can balance my public life with my private life, which is more nurturing."

Some fathers' daughters of powerful men may suffer from the "big man illusion." They identify with their fathers' power, and they believe that, at some level, it belongs to them. They carry the illusion that since their fathers have power and position, they do, too. They expect to be treated with the same respect and deference and are shocked when life does not come easily. Other fathers' daughters constantly compare themselves to their fathers and come up short. Devaluing their own self-worth and power, they feel that no matter what they accomplish, it will never be as worthwhile as their fathers' accomplishments. In both of these cases, the daughter is disempowered; in the first case, she stands on the shifting sands of inflation, and in the second, she is eclipsed by the shadow of her father, the hero.

In my twenties and early thirties, I dismissed my ability to contribute anything of value because what I did was dwarfed by my estimation of my father. He was a *big* man with a big agency, a big house, a big salary, and a big reputation. One night I had a dream in which a voice said, "You are not your father." The voice was direct and clear. I was startled awake by the obvious reality of that statement. I had never consciously explored the idea before, but now I realized that I was certainly living out my inflated view of my father by not acknowledging my own self-worth.

I had created a mythology around him as a "big man" that he unconsciously endorsed. He had power in the outer world, and his lack of genuine interest in my work confirmed my unimportance in comparison to him. My thoughts and opinions held little interest for him; they did not reflect those of the masculine world. I devalued my skills as a teacher and therapist because they seemed relatively insignificant to my father's power as the head of an advertising agency. Instead of acknowledging my skills as valuable, I took them for granted. It wasn't until I started doing what I truly love, which is writing, that I was able to demythologize him and acknowledge my own voice. I then began to realize that his insidious devaluation had not only eroded my self-worth but had undermined my first marriage. Both consciously and unconsciously, I had compared my first husband negatively to my father, particularly in the realm of his ability to provide for us. In frustration he would remind me that he was not my father. It took me a long time to come to terms with how my depreciation of both my husband and myself had contributed to the disintegration of our marriage.

Daughters who grow up with fathers who are "larger than life" discover that having a successful relationship is difficult. A father's daughter often wants a man who appears to have the type of power her idealized father embodied, so she looks for a man with professional status or wealth, but soon she learns that such power alone is a poor substitute for nurturing and compatibility. In the following example, Samantha describes her difficulty with relationships.

"When I was younger, what I thought was so compelling about my father was what other people thought was compelling: He was hip and successful, fun and powerful. After all, he recorded Janis Joplin. So I met a lot of people like that. I married a powerful man who remained a stranger to me. After I married, I realized it wasn't the power that was attractive.

"Now I know that I would like to find a man who respects creativity, and understands what a passion it is, and knows that when you are creating—whatever your passion is—it is more important than your spouse. It is an extension of who you are; it's not a separate thing. Many men view a woman's creativity as threatening, as some kind of power struggle. It's critical for me to be with someone who understands my need for creative expression and isn't belittled by it. I want to find someone who has his own passion I can share in and support as well."

When a woman stops projecting her illusions about power onto the men in her life, she can focus on her own creative potential. She then looks for a spouse who is complementary, not an ideal; a mate who understands the value of both autonomy and emotional connection.

The Phantom Father

The phantom father has just as much power as a father who is present, but his power comes from his *absence* and the *promise of his return*. Although the phantom father is rarely home, his presence is clearly felt, just as an amputee continues to feel the presence of an absent limb. Also like the amputee, who cannot stand on a leg that is not there, the daughter of the phantom father can never rely on her father's support. Some of the deepest pain my women clients have expressed is their sorrow about absent fathers or fathers who made promises they never kept.

Fathers' daughters who are continually disappointed by their phantom fathers react in a variety of ways. If the daughter accepts her father's excuse for his absence as reasonable, she may forgive him, assured that he would be there, *if only he could*. She feels that she has no right to be disappointed or upset. Through cajoling and manipulation, her father virtually tells her to swallow her feelings and accept his view of reality. "You understand, sweetie, don't you? If I could be there, I would. It's just that this business meeting (client, dinner, case, trip, game, political meeting) can't be missed. You understand, I know."

Implied in this statement is the superior importance and value of the father's world over the daughter's world. Father and daughter collude to avoid her sense of disappointment and anger. The daughter cloaks her feelings of abandonment in noble understanding. She accepts her father's importance to the world, which somehow precludes her right to be angry. She also doesn't want to feel the emptiness and pain of her father's seeming indifference.

Another father's daughter will pretend that her father *is* there for her, creating a fantasy about his support, comforting herself with the illusion of his presence. She spends her childhood waiting for the phantom father to return, to listen to her as he does in her fantasies, to spend unhurried time with her, to share her activities. Each time her fantasy is smashed, she tells herself that *next time* will be different. Still another father's daughter will work hard to achieve goals valued by the phantom father in order to attract his attention, while still another will rebel to provoke his response. In adulthood, a daughter whose father was absent may continue to seek his presence in surrogate form by creating situations in which she relies on male support. On the other hand, a daughter who has been repeatedly disappointed by the phantom father may never put her trust in a man again and may turn to a female lover instead.

The internalized phantom father reigns like an overthrown monarch; he rules his daughter's psyche *in absentia*. She continues to uphold the values she knows he supports.

Sylvia's father was an underground organizer for the Communist Party for the first eight years of her life. She lived with her mother, who was the provider for the family, two grandmothers, and her older brother. Her daily world was dominated by women, but her emotional world was dominated by her father's absence.

She says, "Even though we never knew when we were going to see my father, our world revolved around seeing him and not seeing him. He was the dynamic personality, the mover and shaker, the manipulator of events; he was the life giver, our connection to the outside world. We were all fed by his power. He was important because he was doing important things in the world, and therefore we bowed to his every wish. We had no power of our own."

Sylvia's father wanted her to be self-sufficient and repeatedly told her throughout childhood and adolescence that she would have to take full responsibility for herself and her livelihood. However, he never supported her specific talents or aspirations, nor did he convey his confidence in her ability to contribute something of value to the world separate from him. She says, "My father never nurtured my potential; it was insignificant compared to his important work. I grew up in his shadow. When I was thirty, my father announced that he saw me as competent, able, and bright. I remember thinking, This is too late. I sort of believe you, but it's twenty-five years too late. I needed to hear that as a young girl."

If a father has a position of prestige in the world but never encourages his daughter to develop her own potential separate from his, she will remain bound to him and to his image of her. Sylvia continues, "My father never could see me as having an identity and needs of my own. My needs were subsumed to the needs of the Communist Party. When the Party collapsed as a political force and fell into disgrace during the 1950s in the United States, I think my father saw himself as a failure and perceived me through the same lens. Although I'm successful in my career, I've swallowed his image of failure—hook, line, and sinker. I'm not powerful on my own; any power I have is tied to my early image of him as hero in the Communist Party."

Sylvia both resents and admires her father's choice to follow *his political principles even though they involved the sacrifice of family. "I forgive him for not being a great parent," she says, "because he had big, idealistic goals; he helped raise the level of humanity. He made sacrifices for those ideals, and some of that sacrifice was me. But I'm afraid to be mad at my father, or at men in general, for that matter. They'll leave. Getting mad means that I have some of my own desires, expectations, and rights. In our household, there was no space left for the needs of the individual. I shape myself around the air of other people. I have no power in relationships; I have difficulty making my needs known to my boyfriend or even my female friends."*

Redeeming a Father's Powerlessness

C. G. Jung used the term *shadow* to describe the part of the psyche that contains qualities that do not fit neatly into a person's self-image: Most of us, for example, are reluctant to acknowledge that we can be selfish, weak, or full of rage. Jung tells the story of meeting a distinguished gentleman, a Quaker, who could not imagine that he had ever done anything wrong in his life. "And do you know what happened to his children?" Jung asked. "The son became a thief, and the daughter a prostitute. Because the father would not take on his shadow, his share in the imperfection of human nature, his children were compelled to live out the dark side which he had ignored."[17]

Children often "act out" the disowned shadow aspects of one or both parents; this is particularly likely when the shadow qualities of a powerful, weak, or beloved family member are viewed as shameful or intolerable.[18] A father's daughter who has felt her father's buried disappointment, humiliation, and powerlessness may seek to redeem him through her own pursuit of power.

Gretchen, whom we met in chapter 3, is a screenwriter and producer whose career has revolved around trying to realize her father's unfulfilled potential. She is a father's daughter who has always perceived herself as carrying forth her father's destiny. Having recently terminated a ten-year writing partnership with an older man who is very much like her father, she says: "I realized that this entire relationship of ten years was an effort to redeem my father. I felt that if I could work with this man—who had so much potential but such a streak of arrogance, insecurity, and anarchy, very much like my father—and together create something, my frustration with my father would be resolved. My writing partner has an enormous wealth of knowledge, and I felt that if I could just craft that knowledge, twist it around, and put it down on the written page, I could redeem his life. Of course, I also got something out of it. Nevertheless, I can't believe it took me so long to understand what I was doing."

Gretchen's father entered World War II as a young man with a lot of promise but was unable to achieve his goals once he was released from the military. He felt that he had lost ground to the men who had stayed at home and gone to college. He never found fulfillment in his job as an auditor. Gretchen says, "My father is a brilliant man, extremely intelligent, tall, and attractive. He has a photographic memory. He has enormous skills that could have served not only our family life but the community as well. But he has never talked like he wanted to serve anyone. His attitude toward life is 'us versus them.' "

Gretchen's father was an only child in a family whose members believed in their own superiority. Gretchen referred to them as the "fallen royalty"; her father called them the "solid stock" of forefathers who had fought in the American Revolution. The shadow side of her father's inflation and privilege as a young man was his inability to use his talents to achieve power in the world and his bitterness when success did not come easily. The belief that they were people of a superior social class in effect anesthetized members of the family, including Gretchen and her father. Instead of exerting effort and taking risks to get what they wanted, they simply felt entitled to be given whatever they

*desired. Gretchen says, "At thirty-five I had the mentality that
everything was going to come my way because I was one of the
chosen people. It never occurred to me that you have to get out
there and hustle." Her father was not happy in his job, but it allowed him to provide for his family without taking risks. He
never encouraged Gretchen to go after what she wanted; he
never modeled the desire, skills, and drive that one needs to
achieve authority and power.*

*Gretchen began to realize that she had internalized her fa-
ther's fear of actualizing his potential. "I kept myself in failed
situations. I am a very capable person, but I never made a commitment to anything. I took low-paying secretarial jobs I didn't
care about so that I would have more free time despite less
salary. I did a lot of nonprofit work, and I lived hand-to-mouth.
I deliberately lived a poor life-style. I was enormously unsuccess-
ful on many levels. I was living a fairy tale, like Cinderella. Cinderella was supposed to be royal, but she lived in rags. She was
the fallen royalty waiting for someone to come and redeem her.
So was I; I was waiting for my father to finally assume his
proper role of Prince Charming."*

*At thirty-five, Gretchen decided that she had to go out and get
her own "crown." She made a personal commitment to get serious about her film career by getting her movie made, vowing
that if she failed, she would leave the movie business altogether.
"I decided that if I couldn't make it happen by giving it my deepest commitment, by taking the risks to make it happen, then I
was living someone else's life, not my own. If that was true, I
needed to get out of this town and reassess my priorities."*

*Gretchen wrote the script and raised the money to produce her
movie. She was able to accomplish something that is extremely difficult for a woman in the entertainment industry to accomplish,
and this fact changed her life. It also changed her perception of
power. She found that taking action and giving form to her ideas
gave her a deep sense of satisfaction, which was empowering.*

"I have completely redefined power for myself. I'm much

more in touch with internal power now, which has nothing to do with what happens on the surface or who wins an argument in a meeting. Power is a deep current. All the work women have been doing in support groups and organizations in the past years is about finding this internal power. We have looked at what has been advertised as power and what we see as power in a dominating, greedy culture, and that is not true power."

The Death of the Old Order:
King Lear and Cordelia

In order to reclaim her internal power, every father's daughter has to examine the nature of the implicit promise she made with her father in childhood. Gretchen did so when she made a commitment to actualize *her* potential instead of focusing on her father's unlived potential; Brenda did so when she stopped competing with her father and started to write from her heart. Each daughter does it in her own time and at her own risk. In Shakespeare's *King Lear*, the king's favorite daughter, Cordelia, challenges the covenant she made with her father to provide for her always, when she refuses to declare that her love belongs *solely* to him. Her challenge of the covenant provokes her exile by her father and eventually costs her her life.

Shakespeare's play opens as King Lear divides a map of his kingdom into three pieces. He is preparing to abdicate his throne by dividing his land among his three daughters in accordance with each daughter's devotion. He is about to invest each with the privilege of royalty, but he has divided his lands unevenly, wanting to give the largest piece to Cordelia, his favorite daughter. He also wants to ensure his comfort by living with her, along with one hundred of his knights.

Lear demands that each daughter proclaim her love for him in front of the assembled witnesses, thereby fulfilling his condition for bestowing status and wealth upon her in the kingdom. His two oldest daughters, Goneril and Regan, flatter him with exaggerated words of love and devotion and are awarded their share of his property. Goneril says:

> "Sir, I love you more than words can wield the matter;
> Dearer than eye-sight, space, and liberty;
> Beyond what can be valued, rich or rare;
> No less than life, with grace, health, beauty, honor;
> As much as child e'er loved, or father found;
> A love that makes breath poor, and speech unable;
> Beyond all manner of so much I love you."[19]

Regan surpasses her sister's words of love:

> "Sir, I am made
> Of the self-same metal that my sister is,
> And prize me at her worth. In my true heart
> I find she names my very deed of love;
> Only she comes too short: that I profess
> Myself an enemy to all other joys,
> Which the most precious square of sense possesses;
> And find I am alone felicitate
> In your dear highness' love."[20]

Lear's youngest daughter, Cordelia, knows that her sisters' words camouflage hearts hardened by greed and lust for power. Cordelia speaks simply of her love and her bond to her father. Lear asks Cordelia to express her love more lavishly:

> "What can you say to draw
> a third more opulent than your sisters? Speak."
> Cordelia replies, "Nothing, my lord."
> Lear: "Nothing!"
> Cordelia: "Nothing."[21]

Lear is outraged and tells her that nothing will come of nothing. He tells her to speak again. Cordelia replies.

> "Unhappy that I am, I cannot heave
> My heart into my mouth: I love your majesty
> According to my bond; no more nor less."[22]

She cannot adequately describe her love for him in words, and she refuses to flatter him for the sake of flattery. She continues:

> "You have begot me, bred me, loved me: I return
> those duties back as are right fit,
> Obey you, love you, and most honor you.
> Why have my sisters husbands, if they say
> They love you all? Haply, when I shall wed,
> That lord whose hand must take my plight shall carry
> Half my life with him, half my care and duty;
> Sure, I shall never marry like my sisters,
> To love my father all."[23]

Cordelia speaks plainly. She acknowledges her love for Lear as her father but tells him that her love does not belong to him exclusively; someday she will marry and love a husband as well. Lear is devastated. He expected her total love and devotion; instead, she gives him absolute truth, which he cannot tolerate. Lear denounces her, proclaiming that she will inherit nothing. Her third of the land will be absorbed by her two sisters. Lear gives Cordelia in marriage to the sovereign of France, who is willing to accept her without a dowry because he recognizes her integrity. Lear dismisses them both, saying:

> "Thou hast her, France: let her be thine; for we
> Have no such daughter, nor shall ever see
> That face of hers again. Therefore be gone
> Without our grace, our love, our benison."[24]

Because Lear does not get what he wants, he resorts to using his *privilege* as king. Privilege can be enacted by either a beneficent benefactor or a punishing ruler. Lear enacted the punishing, patriarchal king. "Lear acts like a god who can give and take away as he pleases."[25] Afraid to show his vulnerability, Lear rules with will, not with wisdom. (We can almost hear the modern-day patriarchal father say to his daughter, "You can't go out *because I said so*, and I'm your father!")

Lear wishes to return to the womb, to be cared for by his favorite daughter. But he is not direct. He does not ask for what he truly wants; instead he uses his privilege as king. Cordelia challenges his power by disobeying his demand for flattery; acceding to his wishes would be a betrayal of her love for him and her own integrity. Her allegiance is not to the old order of patriarchy but to her own truth. She refuses the ancient feminine role of seducing a man by flattering his ego. Lear, the aging king, cannot tolerate her truthfulness and withdraws his love. Stuck in his world of rules, Lear is arrested psychologically and cannot accept change. He has projected onto Cordelia the image of the perfect, obedient, virginal daughter, but she destroys that image with her simple truth.

Shakespeare's story of King Lear is a story of the patriarchy using manipulation and willpower over the feminine to get what it wants. Lear may step down from the throne, but he does not relinquish his authority. He withholds his love and property when his conditions for that love are denied. Lear's ego still lives under the illusion of great power.

Lear's three daughters represent two aspects of the feminine: treachery and truth. Goneril and Regan return his manipulation in kind, with their own greed for power. They speak the words he wants to hear, proclaiming their love and promising to care for him. When they have what they want, they discard him. Rejected and homeless and devastated by the betrayal of his daughters, Lear loses his senses.

Cordelia eventually returns from France to save her father from the treachery of her sisters, and she joins him in his suffering. Because she brings foreign troops with her to fight the English, she is hung as a traitor. It is only through her death that Lear's illusions are finally shattered and he recognizes the truth of her love. In the last scene, Lear, mad with grief, enters carrying the dead Cordelia. He laments:

> "Howl, howl, howl, howl! O, you are men of stones:
> Had I your tongues and eyes, I'd use them so
> That heaven's vault should crack. She's gone for ever!
> I know when one is dead, and when one lives;
> She's dead as earth."[26]

Lear dies of a broken heart, and his two remaining daughters die as a result of their own jealousy and treachery. Like other loving daughters who seek to redeem their fathers' unrealized potential, Cordelia sacrifices herself for his redemption. Her truth and love redeem his will and hubris. She restores him to sanity and, in the process, becomes a martyr.

This pattern of sacrifice for the patriarchal masculine runs deep in the female psyche. Cordelia is neither the first nor the last heroine in literature to give her life to raise paternal consciousness. This sacrifice is something that we have to examine as women. How long are we willing to abdicate ourselves to redeem the masculine? (And are we willing to make the same sacrifice for the feminine?) The patriarchal masculine psyche, severed from the relational qualities of the feminine, has gained power and domination by force and sheer will, and in the process, living systems have been destroyed. Lear made decisions without consulting his heart, and they were fatal. When the ruling principle, the ego, is disconnected from feeling, there is no true knowledge of self, no consciousness, and no true power. It is only when the mind and the heart work together that there can be harmony and true power.

Women's Power

From an archetypical perspective, women's power is viewed quite differently from men's. It is not external power or *power over*, which is linked to masculine domination, hierarchy, and control, but *power from within*. It is seen as earthy, dark, and bloody. In many native American traditions, menstruating women are not allowed to participate in the ceremonial sweat lodge because of their power during their "moontime." There is power in their blood; not only does a woman purify herself during menstruation, but she also has strong dreams and visions which may be stronger than those of others in the sweat lodge.

In *Truth or Dare*, feminist scholar and spiritual teacher

Starhawk writes that *power from within* "arises from our sense of connection, our bonding with other human beings, and with the environment. Although *power over* rules the systems we live in, *power from within* sustains our lives. We can feel that power in acts of creation and connection, in planting, building, writing, cleaning, healing, soothing, playing, singing, and making love."[27] *Power from within* nurtures.

In cultures, societies, and systems that are defined by a *power over* world view, human beings have no inherent worth of their own. Their value is relative and comparative and must be earned or granted. Our economic system is structured in such a way that some members of society have power while the majority feel dependent on, or subject to, that power. The roots of this inequity are in the family. In the family, power usually resides in the father, whether he is present or not. God as Father is the quintessential archetypal expression of this assignment of power. The *power over* model derives its authority from patriarchal religions that locate God the Father outside the natural world of earth and flesh. His worth surpasses all others, and he must be appeased, placated, obeyed, and worshipped. Above all, his position must be maintained.

In the *power from within* consciousness, value is not earned but inherent. Power is not embodied in an entity that rules from above but is manifest in each person, the community, and nature. It is immanent. Starhawk writes. "Every being is sacred—meaning that each has inherent value that cannot be ranked in a hierarchy or compared to the value of another being. Worth does not have to be earned, acquired, or proven; it is inherent in our existence."[28]

Women who have been reluctant to claim power in the home, workplace, and culture because of negative associations with patriarchal dominance and control are discovering a form of power that is inclusive and fluid and combines relatedness and action. It emphasizes an agenda to be advanced for the purpose of others. It is not the acquisition of power merely for ego gratification. Starhawk writes that this type of power is "the power of a strong individual in a group of equals, the power not to command, but to suggest and be listened to, to begin something and see it happen."[29]

In their study of women in elected office, Dorothy W. Cantor and Toni Bernay define a type of power they call "Woman-Power" embodied by these women in their efforts to effect change. They write, "WomanPower is power used to make society a better place. It is not power for its own sake or for manipulating others."[30] It is an inclusive type of power that combines relatedness with what they define as creative aggression: pulling together resources to advance a specific agenda that helps other people. In doing so, they empower others as well.

As more and more women assume positions of power in the world, fathers' daughters will be called upon to take back the power they have projected onto their fathers and assume responsibility for their own lives. Instead of automatically responding to the internalized voice of the father who rules her psyche, the father's daughter must learn to separate his voice from hers and trust her inner authority. Only then will the covenant she made with her father no longer bind her; only then will she begin to accept the full responsibility that power entails.

Womanspirit Emerging by Maureen Murdock.
(Black & white photograph, 11 × 14 in., 1992.
Reprinted by permission of the artist.)

CHAPTER SEVEN

Women and Spirituality

Our Father who art in Heaven, hallowed be Thy Name. Thy
Kingdom come, Thy will be done, on earth as it is in Heaven.
—The Lord's Prayer

A DAUGHTER'S relationship with her father influences
her spiritual beliefs about the nature of the universe and her perception of a godhead. Whether or not her father has a strong relationship to his own spirituality, the fact that he embodies the Father
archetype greatly affects how his daughter will view God. If her
father is loving and accessible, God will be viewed as loving and
accessible, too. If she observes her father living his life with compassion, without hypocrisy, hers will be a fair, compassionate God.
If her father is protective and benevolent, her God will protect her,
too. If her father ignores her and fails to protect her, her God may
be an abandoning, impotent deity. If her father betrays her through
his absence, abuse, or death, her God will carry the threat of betrayal. If he is indifferent to religion but lives his life with integrity,
she will adopt his judicious, secular values.

In *King, Warrior, Magician, Lover*, Robert Moore and Douglas Gillette write, "The King archetype comes close to being God

in his masculine form within every man."[1] As the embodiment of the King archetype, the father is the mediator between the divine world and the earthly kingdom, between God and his family. God is at the center of the universe, and from this central place all creation radiates. God as Center is a recurring theme throughout most religions and mythologies. The King's first responsibility is to embody the mysterious "right order" of the universe—the ordering, generative, creative precepts of God. If the king does so, his kingdom will flourish; if he does not, nothing will go right for his people.[2] As an embodiment of the King's energy in its positive form (the wise king), the father embodies this "right order" for his family, providing for the prosperity of his family and affirming and supporting the worth of its members.

When the father embodies negative aspects of the King archetype (the patriarchal king), he will be revered and feared like the Old Testament God, Yahweh, whose word is absolute. Likewise, the father's authority is rarely questioned. Remote and inaccessible, he metes out approval and punishment as he sees fit. In this type of family the father is the central, dominating figure; his wife is secondary, and his children's status is determined by birth order and gender. His female children serve as little more than handmaidens who are there to listen, obey, and never disappoint him.

Nancy, whom we met in chapter 2, had a father who embodied the Wise King archetype, not only in the family but in the community as well. Serving as the president of the Jewish temple to which the family belonged, he was very involved in the social life that revolved around temple politics. He was at the center of this group, and his power in it defined the family's social status. Nancy remembers how she associated the prayers and music of the temple with her father. Whenever she listened to the rabbi chant, "Aveenu, Malkaynu, Our Father, Our King," she thought of her father as the king, lord, ruler, and center of the universe.

Nancy's father died in a diving accident when she was eleven.

With his death, the family not only lost its center but was displaced from the inner circle of the temple; the women in the family had no value in the temple without the father. When Nancy lost her father, she lost her belief in God. Her father had embodied the archetype of the King so strongly that when he died, God died, too.

In most families it is the mother who makes spirituality tangible by preserving and honoring the spiritual traditions and rituals that are passed on to succeeding generations. However, it is the father as inheritor of the King/God archetype who determines the spiritual "right order," or lack thereof, in the family. The father's spiritual legacy is conveyed both explicitly and implicitly. In *The Feminine Face of God*, Marion Woodman writes about the explicit support she received as a child from her minister father to explore spirituality in her own way. She recalls that when she was a little girl, her father accepted her conversations with angels. "You see, he was a Scotsman who had been brought up in a culture which accepted nature spirits. So even though he was a minister, he had no problem at all with my angels. He accepted them."[3] Woodman continues:

> Like many children, I was very intuitive. I would say things like, "You know, somebody has been fighting here." Or I would look at our hostess and say, "You don't like your husband very much, do you?" And then there would be this horrible silence. As soon as we'd leave my father would take me aside and say, "Marion, it's not that I don't want you to speak, but you say things that are simply not acceptable in society. It's all right for you to tell me these things, but you must not say them to other people."[4]

Woodman's father acknowledged and encouraged her relationship with angels but knew that others would be less accepting. His explicit acceptance of her childhood spirituality gave Woodman a foundation that helped her enter into a mature spirituality in adulthood. As an adult, she renewed an interest in organized religion through study and practice of the rituals of the

Anglican church and also came to understand an embodied sense of spirituality as a woman.

An example of implicit communication of spirituality is provided by the father who inadvertently conveys spiritual values by showing his daughter how to relate to nature in an appreciative and respectful way. As one such daughter said: "My father had a profound effect on me spiritually. He loved being outdoors; he loved the mountains. He didn't give me words of wisdom; he didn't teach me how to succeed in the business world. But he took me *there*—to the mountains. He taught me to be responsible when we went camping and to leave a place cleaner than when I came. I grew up with a very deep connection to nature."

Fathers' Daughters and Spirituality

A father's daughter's relationship with her father influences her perception of God and her spiritual values to an even greater degree than the type of father-daughter relationship in which the father is not idealized. The idealization of the father occupies the father's daughter's psyche with a potency that infuses every aspect of her life. Most of the women I interviewed reported that their fathers (unless they were ministers) did not explicitly teach them about spiritual issues, but that the way in which their fathers chose to live their lives implied these values in one way or another. The force of the father's personality and the fact that he is the center of his daughter's universe invariably permeate her cosmological point of view. One woman told me that, in her late teens, she travelled to Beirut during a politically explosive time and felt no fear for her safety. Because her father had been protective and benevolent, she assumed that the rest of the world would protect and assist her, too. As in all father-daughter relationships, the father's daughter receives either implicit or explicit messages about spirituality.

Connie, a ceramicist and mother in her early forties, is a father's daughter whose father, "a New Testament, sweet-Jesus type of minister" from a small Methodist community in West Texas, gave her quite explicit messages. He was her first spiritual teacher, her first gateway to the realm of the sacred. Her earliest memory is one of talking with her father about God:

"I was not quite three years old, and we were in the yard lying on our backs watching the stars pop out. I asked him, 'Who made the stars?' and my father said, 'God did.' I replied, 'God must be really big,' and he said, 'Yes, God is big.' "

Connie's father imparted to her teachings of the New Testament, which became the cornerstone of her subsequent spiritual studies. He articulated a set of rules delineated by the church, which he expected her to obey. Connie argued with him about the rules, but she never argued with him about his behavior. She respected the fact that he lived according to the rules he believed in. She learned from him to "walk your talk."

"Where we differ is that I see the walk *and the* talk *as mutually important. If I find myself doing something that I don't believe in, I have to reevaluate that belief. He would simply call the aberrant behavior a sin and ask for forgiveness." In adolescence, Connie found her father's belief system too limiting and even injurious to her when she repeatedly asked him for help in dealing with her mother's angry, abusive behavior. Her father ignored her pleas for counseling, instead remonstrating her to "honor and obey" her mother.*

Connie attended college at a Methodist university, but as an adult she left the church and developed an interest in native American spirituality. She is now apprenticed to another "father," a Tewa medicine man whose only requirement is that, through their work together, she "fall more and more in love with life every day."

She says, "I left the church of my father, but I never left my basic belief in the truth of the teachings of Christ that my father taught me: Love your neighbor; give your life to gain it; death is

*not what you think it is; and transformation is absolutely real
and possible. He gave me an enormous foundation, and when I
eventually encountered native American teachings, I found them
to be in total alignment with what I had been taught as a young
child. So, ironically, my father helped me make the connections
that eventually led to my spiritual path—which was very different
from his spiritual path. If he had been able to teach me that we
must "fall more and more in love with life every day" in order to
understand spirit, my whole life would have been different."*

A father's daughter looks to her father not only for his guidance about how to live life, but also for concrete explanations
about the mysteries of life. If her father has no interpretation of
these mysteries, his daughter will feel disappointed and confused, since his lack of input conflicts with her image of him as
all-knowing. Jennifer, whom we met in chapter 4, finds this one
flaw with her father:

*"The one area in which my father let me down was the spiri-
tual department. He had a bad experience in Catholic school
when he was a child, and he didn't want his kids to go through
that same experience. But I wanted to be Catholic—I still do! I
was baptized Catholic, and although I don't believe in all the
church's positions on social issues, I accept many of the teachings—especially about death and afterlife. A friend's father died
recently, and I have been thinking a lot about what happens after death. Part of my understanding about life is that there's
something beyond my physical being. My father didn't discuss
these kinds of ideas. I think he has mixed feelings."*

My own father and I rarely discussed spiritual issues, but his
love for his garden, his respect for nature, and the generous way
with which he treated his employees implied his spiritual values.
He did, however, help me dispel any associations with a punishing, all-powerful God. The father of my childhood was always
very easygoing, not an authoritarian figure, and not the type of

man who enforced rules. In fact, as a creative person, he made up his own rules. So I didn't have a visceral experience of the wrathful Old Testament God that I heard about from classmates in my Catholic grade school who were spanked in God's name. I actually didn't have much of a relationship with God per se, because he seemed so remote. I consistently prayed to him for help with my mother, but since he never intervened, I figured he was too busy to listen. Perhaps, too, because of my father's unresponsiveness in this same area, I dismissed God as being inaccessible and ineffectual. I projected my sense of the divine, instead, onto the Virgin Mary, whom I unconsciously viewed as the beautiful, loving, compassionate, positive mother I wished for myself.

The positive side of my father's spiritual indifference was his irreverence, which spared me from the tortured clutches of obedience to dogma. One day in second grade, it was my turn to take home the classroom statue of Mary that came with glow-in-the-dark rosary beads. Mary went home on a rotating schedule so that each student could recite the rosary with her family. That night my mother had to go to a meeting, so she asked my father to kneel with me and recite the rosary. We knelt in front of the statue of Mary, which I had placed on my bedside table. I was skeptical about my father's knowledge of the prayers, but he mumbled along in what seemed to be the correct ryhthm. I acquired a terrible case of hiccoughs, so I couldn't really hear him anyway. The room was dark except for the light emanating from Mary and the beads moving in my hands. I kept waiting for Mary to move or to smile. My hiccoughs just got louder and louder. All of a sudden my father shouted, "Boo!" and I jumped, laughing and crying at the same time. I didn't want Mary to think my father was disrespectful, because then he would never get to heaven. But his irreverence somehow relieved me from the onus of being holy and got rid of my hiccoughs at the same time. I realized much later that, along with my father's irreverence, I also absorbed his relaxed attitude about the rules and dogma of the church. Not all fathers' daughters are as fortunate.

Betrayal by God Through Religious Hierarchies

Fathers' daughters grow up assuming that they will share in their fathers' status and power as adults. Many also grow up following the doctrines and dogma of male priests, rabbis, or ministers. Fathers' daughters who blindly follow church doctrine and dogma are still adhering to the unspoken covenant they made in childhood with their fathers to be protected and loved. As they grow into adulthood, they continue to "serve" husbands, sons, and bosses, lacking the inner focus to serve the Self within them. On one hand, fathers' daughters grow up assuming a superior position; on the other hand, they unconsciously accept their role as handmaidens to male authority figures.

Patriarchal religions preserve the image of God as male and, with this, ensure the privilege of the male hierarchy. Many of the men who have such positions of power are interested only in women who wish to serve the status quo, not in women who want to join their ranks. In *Laughter of Aphrodite*, theologian Carol Christ describes her surprise and disillusionment in finding out that her personal status as a father's daughter was not sufficient to grant her equal hierarchical status in her church, nor did it win her the approval of the male professors with whom she studied the Bible. She writes:

> I assumed that I could be the favored child of the Father if I figured out how to please him. It never occurred to me to question whether daughters could ever find an equal place in the house of the Father. Despite the pathological elements in my relationships with fathers, I did gain confidence in my own intelligence and abilities through their support. I gained a degree of freedom from traditional female roles by imagining a core of self that transcended femaleness. I assumed that the God whose words I would study transcended the genderized language of the Bible. I thought I could become like my male professors because we shared a common humanity, defined by our love for the intellectual life, our interest in religious questions.[5]

Carol was flattered when she was told that she "thought like a man"; she felt special, like a favored daughter. She had contempt for women who were satisfied to fill traditional women's roles, realizing only later that this attitude amounted to a betrayal of her own femaleness. Modeling herself on the Father and male mentors left her clueless as to how to think like a woman or how to empathize with other women in their common plight of living in a patriarchal society.

Carol's relationship to the fathers changed in graduate school when she moved from a coeducational college to a predominantly male Eastern university and found difficulty gaining acceptance as an equal colleague-in-training. She writes, "In graduate school I found that I was viewed first as a woman by the men with whom I studied. The nonacceptance of me as a colleague was the catalyst that made me begin to question whether or not daughters could ever be accepted in the house of the fathers."[6] Over time, through this initially disheartening experience, she realized that she was not dependent on God the Father—or any man—for validation of herself as a person, woman, scholar, or teacher. This revelation, in turn, opened her to experiencing the sacredness of the feminine.

Similarly, it is often through a profound disillusionment in the father-daughter covenant that a father's daughter comes to a greater understanding of her spiritual nature as a woman. My own disillusionment with the Catholic Church occurred when I went to Mexico as a junior in college to work with a lay missionary group. I worked with the Huastecan Indians, who were oppressed by poverty and treated as little more than animals by the Mexican government and the church as well. As many people in the mountain village where I worked died from malnutrition and lung disease, I pleaded with the Catholic bishop to intercede with the Mexican government for decent health care. He smiled indulgently at my youthful idealism and told me that this was not part of God's plan. He didn't bother to explain how a fair, benevolent God could manage to install *him* in a grand mansion with plumbing and television while the Indians continued to live with their pigs in mud huts. When I questioned whether this inequity was part of God's plan, my audience with him was abruptly terminated. I was stunned by his dismissal. Despite the fact that I knew women did not question religious authority in Latin cultures, with my heritage as a father's daughter I expected to be listened to; I expected to be able to effect change. It was then that I began to understand, and later name, the power and injustice of patriarchal hierarchies that support economic systems that exploit women, children, indigenous peoples, and the land. I also began to understand that even though the sun shone on me in my father's eyes, this did not translate to the world at large.

Spiritual Daughters of the Patriarchy

Of all father-daughter relationships, the one that most embodies and perpetuates the worship of the father (the patriarchy) and the denial of the mother (the feminine) is the one between a father and a father's daughter. As fathers' daughters, we need to educate ourselves so that, in our identification with the father, we do not unwittingly perpetuate oppressive ideologies that deny the divinity of the feminine. In my late thirties I became interested in Goddess-centered cultures and in the idea that the divine was immanent, rather than confined to a supreme male deity. I was riveted by the powerful images of the divine feminine depicted by various cultures. The idea of God as a woman, not solely (as I had been taught) as a man, was both liberating and exhilarating. It meant that the feminine was sacred and had equal status with the masculine. It also meant that, as a woman, I was no longer separate from God and that, as a daughter, I did not have to identify with my father to know God.

I spent the next two years photographing women from different socioeconomic and ethnic groups and interviewing them about their personal understandings of the Goddess and what part she played in their lives. This project, entitled "Changing Woman: Contemporary Faces of the Goddess," was the focus of a cable television program. When I played the videotape of the program for my parents, my father, perplexed by the idea of God embodied in a female form, bellowed, "*Who* is this Goddess?" and "That can't possibly be *my* daughter spouting such nonsense!" The idea of a supreme female deity was just as unacceptable to my father as it would be to the pope. I was dumbstruck by his response. Only later did I feel annoyed that he had completely dismissed something that I valued so highly, and that he hadn't been able to put his views aside, even momentarily, to appreciate my accomplishment. My father's response also made it clear that we could never discuss any interest of mine that did not reflect his values. If I wanted to pursue my exploration of the divine feminine, I would have to sever the covenant we made in which *he* is the supreme deity in my world.

In *The Politics of Women's Spirituality*, feminist scholar Charlene Spretnak asks an intriguing question: What would happen if it were known by all women and all men that the patriarchy was only a couple of thousand years old, and that for the preceding twenty-five thousand years societies were built around the concept of the Great Goddess? Would patriarchal religions and social structures continue to be perceived as the natural order of things? Would women continue to give their power to men? Or, knowing that the father-religions were a relatively recent historical phenomenon, would women begin to assert their equality and reclaim their own divine wisdom?[7]

Through the extensive work of archeologist Marija Gimbutas and numerous other researchers and scholars, knowledge of God the Mother or the Great Goddess, who *predated* the father gods, is becoming widespread. I was fascinated to read that sculptures found in Paleolithic caves, on the open plains of Anatolia, and at other Near Eastern and Middle Eastern Neolithic sites show that the worship of the Goddess was central to all life at least six thousand years ago and, in all probability, up to twenty-five thousand years ago. Sculptures of female figures and symbols occupied a central place in the cave sites, indicating the predominance of the Great Goddess in daily life. Symbols of nature—sun, water, bulls, birds, fish, serpents, cosmic eggs, butterflies, and images of the Goddess both pregnant and giving birth—have been found everywhere in shrines and houses, on vases and clay figurines.[8] In Goddess-centered societies, there was no separation between the secular and the sacred; religion was life and life was religion. The head of the holy family was a woman: the Great Mother. She was held in awe as the Creator. Her body was sacred; all life emanated from her, and the earth as a symbol became synonymous with the female body.

The symbol of the Great Mother as the fertile creator of the earth, often portrayed with a consort or a son, was usurped by the father gods during the barbarian Kurgan invasions and completely eradicated by Christianity's successful attempt to eliminate the Mother archetype and replace her with Father as Creator and Son as Redeemer.[9] Male gods (as omnipotent rulers, rather than as sons or consorts of the Goddess) were introduced in India, the Middle and Near East, Eastern Europe, and later Greece, by invaders who spread out in waves from the Eurasian steppes, beginning around 4500 B.C.[10]

Patriarchal religion, therefore, is a relatively recent phenomenon. The expulsion of the mythological Eve from the Garden of Eden symbolizes the inception of patriarchal domination. Charlene Spretnak writes, "The underlying rationale for patriarchal societies is patriarchal religion. Christianity, Judaism, Islam, and Hinduism all combine male godheads with the proscriptions against woman as temptress, as unclean, as evil. We were made to understand that Eve's act of heeding the word of the serpent caused the expulsion of the human race from the Garden of Eden. We were made to understand that, as a result of her act, it was decreed by God that woman must submit to the dominance of man."[11]

The early rabbinic commentators and fathers of the Church blamed Eve, and thus all women, for bringing death to mankind by disobeying God.[12] Early Church fathers actually established the "fact" that women lack a soul and that the soul is transmitted to a child through her father's semen.[13] This is not such an antiquated belief. Connie, whose father is the Methodist minister mentioned earlier, says, "I just found out that my father always believed that women didn't have souls. He thought it was his responsibility to get my mother, my two sisters, and me into heaven!"

Eve was rejected for disobeying God's rules; she did not serve God perfectly. Like Eve, the Mother of us all, the mother of a father's daughter is rejected by her daughter for not serving the father perfectly; and the daughter, if she dares to deviate from the terms of the covenant, is in turn rejected by the father. We can see how the denigration of the sacred feminine in these larger mythic realities, like the story of Eve, is experienced in current life by looking at the dreams of contemporary women. One father's daughter, raised Episcopalian, described a dream she had when she first joined a women's group to study the Goddess:

> I have created a sacred circle of stones outside and have placed Kwan Yin, the goddess of compassion, in the center. My father comes out to the circle at night when we are not there. He weaves as he walks around the circle, and then he throws an empty Jack Daniel's bottle into the center of the circle, smashing it.

The father in this dream cannot actually enter the women's circle; he can only waver on the periphery. In his alienation, he denigrates and destroys the circle. The loss of the mother religions for women has been a loss for men, too; patriarchal religions have had a devastating effect on everyone. This father's daughter took her first step toward an autonomous spiritual identity when she dreamed of Kwan Yin, instead of a male deity, as the *center* of the circle. In her dream, her father destroys the symbols of a feminine form of worship. This symbolizes the fear she feels as a father's daughter in attempting to dethrone her father by relinquishing her idealization of him. This terror has two sources: the irrational fear an individual father's daughter may have that she could cause her father's death by individuating from him, as we saw in chapter 1 in my own dream about writing this book; and the inherited collective fear that women feel about the consequences of challenging patriarchal religions (which is ultimately necessary for the true divine masculine to emerge).

Embodied Spirituality

Spirit is the unknowable, the unfathomable, that which cannot be described with words. It has most often been depicted in myth and image as Father Sky, Mother Earth, breath, or wind; without spirit, no creation can occur. For creation to take place, spirit must enter the heart, the mind, the *body*. Transformation is possible only when spirit is *embodied*. For fathers' daughters, it is particularly difficult to experience this aspect of embodied spirituality because their identification with their fathers, and the subsequent denial of their mothers, separates them from their feminine nature. By identifying with their fathers, their primary focus becomes the mind, not the body. Nancy experienced vaginal infections while pursuing a high-powered career as a lawyer that did not serve her soul; Marianne neutralized her sexuality in her twenties and early thirties while she immersed herself in Eastern religions; and I almost lost my second pregnancy in my sixth month because I ignored the painful messages I was receiving from my "incompetent" cervix. Each one of us ignored the wisdom of our bodies.

For many women, their most sacred moments have been physical ones: being held, giving a massage, making love, nursing a child, feeling the breath of life expire from a loved one in death. Many women speak of giving birth as entering into the sacred dimension in a way they had never known before. In *The Feminine Face of God*, psychiatrist and Jungian analyst Jean Shinoda Bolen recounts her experience of giving birth as "embodied revelation":

> Something I do not have words for happened during that instant of transition. The self that was familiar seemed to descend into a warm, dark pool and dissolve, and in that moment there was a knowing of the sacred through my body. I participated in the miracle of creation and it shifted my consciousness. It changed me.[14]

The embodied experience of the sacred is certainly not limited to a woman's experience of giving birth. In novelist Alice Walker's *The Color Purple*, Shug Avery gives a superb description of her experience of God in nature, in response to Celie's announcement that she has stopped writing letters to God because "He's triflin', forgitful and lowdown," like all the other men in her life. Shug says:

> God ain't a he or a she, but a It. Don't look like nothing, she say. It ain't a picture show. It ain't something you can look at apart from anything else, including yourself. I believe God is everything, say Shug. Everything that is or ever was or ever will be. And when you see that, and be happy to feel that, you've found it. . . . My first step from the old white man was trees. Then air. Then birds. Then other people. But one day when I was sitting quiet and feeling like a motherless child, which I was, it come to me: *that feeling of being part of everything, not separate at all. I knew that if I cut a tree, my arm would bleed.* And I laughed and I cried and I run all around the house.[15] [italics added]

This feeling of being part of everything is central to spiritual experience. The problem for a father's daughter is that her personal experience is one of *not* being separate, and her developmental task is to differentiate herself from her father. It is only after she has reestablished her boundaries and carved out her own identity that she will have a strong enough core to become *part of everything*—to allow spiritual merger rather than personal engulfment by the father.

Changing Perceptions of God

Our image of God evolves throughout our lives as we seek to comprehend spirituality in our own terms. A more mature understanding occurs for a father's daughter only as she is able to separate her father from her perception of God and experience a more embodied sense of spirituality. Then she can come to know the sacred as immanent, present in both seen and unseen realms. In the following dream, Connie's perception of herself and her father (a fundamentalist minister) changes as she herself experiences the unfathomable. Spirit enters her, she levitates, and she "knows herself" as one of the "sacred women." She dreams:

I am walking on a street when I notice a fundamentalist church I have never seen before. I enter. A man is preaching in a fervent pitch. Most of the people are African-American, and the service is really fun. They sing a rousing rendition of "Rock of Ages." I stay and watch everyone leave; they are so interesting-looking, very peaceful and beautiful. The black minister comes to the back; he is dressed in khaki shorts and looks ready for a safari. I ask him if there will be a service next week. He says that next week is a training period for the "sacred women." I ask who the sacred women are, and he answers curtly, "They are born that way." He is unfriendly, his manner, rude. I decide to drop it; perhaps I'll come back, perhaps not.

As I walk down the steps toward the sidewalk something happens as I walk. I levitate between steps. I step . . . push off . . . float . . . step. It is very graceful, like gravity-free walking. I don't think anyone is noticing, so I just enjoy the sensation. The minister comes down to the sidewalk. He has noticed. There is an open grave next to the sidewalk, and he lays down in it. Suddenly it is his funeral, and the congregation gathers around him. I continue to levitate. He watches me very carefully.

He says, "You're under thirty, aren't you?" The way he says this makes me "dream know" that the sacred women are all un-

*der thirty and that he is considering inviting me to the retreat. I
answer, "No, closer to forty than thirty." He asks if I have had a
facelift. I realize then that he has not actually seen me levitate; he
just thinks there is something about me that is young.*

*I sit down by his grave and say, "No, lots and lots of good
lives." I'm not sure a fundamentalist preacher is ready for a rein-
carnation remark. I say, "You know how it is—you live well and
die well, and then life treats you well the next time. After a few
good deaths, you're on easy street."*

This dream heralded a turning point in Connie's relationship
with the Church and her father, both internalized as sources of
authority. Her earlier dreams typically depicted her as adhering
to church rules, obeying her father, and seeking his protection.
In this dream, she transcends all conformity by levitating; she is
filled with spirit, light, and buoyancy. The minister acknowledges her transformation and lies down in his grave to die. As he
is dying, he spontaneously changes his beliefs about what constitutes a sacred woman.

Connie's own father has not experienced this expansion in his
beliefs, but she hopes he will before he dies. He held rigidly to
church teachings his entire life but was repeatedly disappointed
by the lack of recognition he received from church elders for his
work. He is dying now and feels alienated from his faith.

Connie says: "When I went home, I asked him how he felt, spiritually, and he said, 'Lost.' I asked if he still had feelings about
death, and heaven being a reward, and he said, 'I just don't know';
then he began to cry. I think he has confused church dogma with
spirituality. He's ending his years in a spiritual void."

Connie's father taught her that what a person does with his
life determines whether or not he will get into heaven and receive
his reward. Since his own life's work was not recognized by the
church hierarchy, he is not certain that a reward awaits him in
heaven. She says, "I hope he can let go of this belief system that
has held him captive for so long. But there is no opening now; he
doesn't want me to help him."

Unlike Connie, some fathers' daughters find that, as their fathers approach death, they *want* to communicate with them about spiritual matters; they recognize and *want* to hear their daughters' wisdom. A father's daughter may also find that, as she comes to terms with her father's aging and death, her perception of God changes. As her father loses his heroic image, there is room for a deeper understanding of spirit.

Nancy recently went to her father's grave for the first time since he drowned twenty-one years ago. This visit was prompted by a dream several months before, in which she carried her father's body across a bridge to a grassy knoll and told him that it was time for him to rest. He agreed, so she lay him down in an open grave and said good-bye. Since this poignant dream, Nancy has experienced a renewed interest in Judaism. In a letter to me she wrote:

"As you know, I lost faith when my father, my king—Aveenu, Malkaynu—died. The day my father drowned, God died for me. Within the past year or so, however, I've come to believe in the possibility of a spiritual force beyond humankind. I've spent some time looking into Eastern religions, but I've come to realize that, for better or worse, Judaism is imprinted on my soul— its songs and prayers are the ones that ring an emotional chord. So I've been taking a class on Judaism offered at a local temple by a wonderful, wise old rabbi, reading a lot of literature, and trying to see if there is a way to reconcile the religion of my heritage with my feelings of spirituality. I don't know where this resurgent interest in Judaism will take me. Somehow, by leaving my religion, I cut off the part of myself that was inextricably connected with the loss of my father. Now that I'm strong enough to deal with that loss, and willing to make a new beginning by myself, hopefully I can reincorporate the lost part of Judaism into my life and finally satisfy my spiritual longing."

Both Connie and Nancy have found teachers—a Tewa medicine man and a wise old rabbi, respectively—who embody the "wise old man" archetype who serves as a guide for women to reclaim their spiritual, intuitive natures. But first, both women had to separate from their enmeshment with their fathers to be free to pursue their own interests and beliefs in every arena of their lives. Each had to come to terms with her attachment to her father and begin the painful process of individuating from him. As we shall see in the next chapter, a daughter pays a dear price for abdicating her role as father's daughter in that she must relinquish the privileges and pleasures of remaining the archetypal daughter.

PART III

Reconciliation of the Two

Still Life: Litchfield #1 by Ann W. Glover.
(Oil on panel, 20 × 30 in., 1987–88.
Reprinted by permission of the artist.)

CHAPTER EIGHT

No Longer My Father's Daughter

The root of the conflict is deceptively simple: you long to be
free *and* to be loved. When the first man in your life teaches
you that the two are irreconcilable, the price of freedom can
seem impossibly high.
—Eileen Fairweather, "The Man in the Orange Box"

If we leave our father's house, we have to make ourselves
self-reliant. Otherwise we just fall into another father's house.
—Marion Woodman, *Leaving My Father's House*

A<small>T SOME</small> point during her development into mature
adulthood, a father's daughter must outgrow her psychological
dependence on her father in order to live a healthy, emotionally
connected, yet autonomous life. For most fathers' daughters, this
requires a painful process of separation and individuation. The
attachment to the father is so deep and the fear of losing him is
so great that they cannot imagine any change in the relationship.
Poet Sharon Olds describes the powerful hold of this bond in
"Last Words": "I will not let thee go except thou beg for it."[1]

A father's daughter has experienced a far more intense relationship with her father than with her mother, so her work of

separation is primarily centered on her father. Mother has been "the other woman," viewed by her daughter as cold, distant, non-nurturing, passive, troubled, interfering, or rejecting. However, as a father's daughter examines her relationship with her father, she may begin to understand her mother more clearly. Yet even this new understanding does not guarantee separation from the father. In *Writing a Woman's Life*, Carolyn G. Heilbrun notes, "Mothers may come to be recognized with a new, loving perception, but it is not mothers who free women from their fathers."[2] Still, healing the split between her mother and herself may ease a daughter's separation from her father, because it is easier to let go of him when compassion for her mother has helped her to see that her father is not infallible.

The process of separation for each daughter and father is always unique, and in most cases the daughter is the agent of change, if any change is to be made. The first step toward separation is to consciously acknowledge the degree of attachment.

Marianne says, "I don't know if I'll ever be able to separate from my father. When he goes out of town, I feel his absence, and when he comes home, I light up just knowing that he's back in town. I still need his physical presence." Expressing a similar bond, Chelsea fears that she may never truly be herself until her father dies. Despite the fact that she is now married and has a successful career, her father influences so many of her opinions, feelings, and choices that she wonders who she would be without him. She laments, "I don't want my father to have to die in order for me to be *me*."

Twenty-five-year-old Jennifer admits that her need for her father makes her uneasy. "I still want my father's love, attention, and approval. I need his presence too much. I feel like I'm too close to him. My best friend's father passed away last year, and although she wasn't as close to her father as I am to mine, it was horrible watching her go through the loss. I just don't want to live my life without my father. He's a huge part of it."

Michele's father comforts her when she expresses her fear of losing him. At twenty-eight, she is still living at home with her single father and is troubled by his aging. "He's getting older, and it scares me to think of him not being here. I've talked to him about it, and he assures me that, at that point, I will have my own family and I'll be okay. But it hurts just thinking about it. I can talk to him about everything, and I have his support in any situation."

There are culturally accepted rituals that mark a daughter's leave-taking from her parents in adolescence and early adulthood, but the process of psychological separation remains, for many, a lifelong task. A daughter physically separates from her father when she leaves home for college, work, or travel, moves into her first apartment, buys a house, or gets married. Her father is replaced as her first love only when she enters into her first serious relationship; when she begins to bear children, the physical displacement is literally embodied in grandchildren.

When the bond between father and daughter is particularly enmeshed, as it is for fathers' daughters, ending emotional dependency does not happen through normal developmental stages but occurs only through acts of rejection, rebellion, betrayal, or mutual disappointment. When either the father or daughter fails to live up to the unspoken terms of the childhood covenant, both may be hurt and disappointed. A daughter may make life choices with which her father disagrees and so he rejects her, or he may refuse to relinquish control of her life, forcing her to reject him. A father may feel betrayed (quite unconsciously) when his daughter chooses a spouse, and a daughter who is married or living independently may feel abandoned when her father no longer gives her the continued attention she has come to expect from him. Both father and daughter have projected inflated images on each other that contain unconscious promises neither can keep. Both remain emotionally arrested until they move beyond these projections.

Obstacles to Separating from
a Father

A father's daughter does not want to examine her relationship with her father because she does not want to give up her fantasy of having the perfect relationship with him. In *Women and Their Fathers*, Victoria Secunda writes, "The first hazard of seeing the real man with all his imperfections is that it forces you to separate from him emotionally and give up the rosy notion that he can fix anything, do anything, is an all-powerful hero."[3] If a daughter looks too closely, she might be forced to confront what she did not receive from her father as well as face the emptiness of her relationship with her mother. If she deflates her image of him, she will also have to find out who she is apart from her reflection of him.

In *The Wizard of Oz*, Dorothy and her dog, Toto, are on a quest to return home. In most mythological journeys, *home* represents the universal longing to return to our beginnings; it is the search for the Self, the soul, one's center. Dorothy is a girl without a father who projects all of her hopes, trust, and expectations onto the Great Oz. When she meets Scarecrow, Tinman, and Lion, who are searching for a brain, a heart, and courage, respectively, she convinces them that the Great Oz will help them, too. Dorothy assures them knowingly, "The wizard will fix *everything*."

When Dorothy unmasks Oz and discovers that he is merely a man, not an all-powerful wizard, she is furious at the deception and outraged that he does not have the power to save them. She says, "If you were really great and powerful, you would keep your promise!" She calls him a bad man, but he corrects her, "I'm a very good man—I'm just a very bad wizard." Oz now plays the role of the wise father as he helps Dorothy and her companions realize that what they have sought has been theirs all along. Despite his flaws, Oz is a catalyst for their growth and individuation.

In unmasking the father and accepting his humanness, many fathers' daughters make a journey similar to Dorothy's, demythologizing the myth and accepting the man, flaws and gifts alike. As a child, a father's daughter has an inflated image of her father. He, like the Wizard of Oz, is perceived as all-knowing, all-loving, all-powerful; she takes great joy in recounting tales of his heroism to anyone who will listen ("*My* daddy . . ."). By early adulthood, however, the father's daughter begins to discover that her father cannot give her the heart, the courage, or the brain that she had believed were his to impart. These are attributes that she can develop only within herself. Like Dorothy, she becomes angry with her father when she realizes he cannot deliver the goods. And weren't those goods part and parcel of their covenant? In unmasking her father by removing her childhood projections, a father's daughter must find her own worth and give her father leave to live his own life.

A woman does not separate from her father until she is willing to let go of the privilege of being "Daddy's little girl." Although this special role netted both emotional and financial rewards, it also has required her continued dependence upon his approval, opinions, choices, and perhaps even his checkbook. When a daughter first relinquishes this privilege, she feels empty, isolated, and frightened; her identity is no longer tied to his, and her emotional "rug" has been pulled out from under her. During this painful process, she must allow her father to descend from the pedestal upon which she has kept him enshrined. But to be complete, this process must be mutual; not only must the daughter accept her father as he is, but the father must also accept his daughter as she is. *Both* must reclaim their projections. If this task is accomplished, the daughter learns to trust that she can make her own decisions and provide for herself without her father's approval, and the father begins to develop a new relationship to his own emotions, which his daughter has carried most of her life. None of this occurs without mutual grief.

Keeping a Daughter Attached

The process of separating from a daughter is painful and difficult for a father as well. Their enmeshment has given him considerable control over his daughter's life—control that he may not be prepared to relinquish, for his role as protector and provider has been a satisfying one, indeed. He does not want to lose her love and adulation; her singular devotion to him soothes his aging ego, particularly if his relationship with his wife lacks tenderness and care. He still feels young, vital, and cherished by his "little girl." In the 1940 film *The Philadelphia Story*, the father tells his daughter (played by a modern-day symbol of the independent woman, Katharine Hepburn): "The best mainstay a man has as he gets on in years is a daughter, the right kind of daughter. . . . The devoted young girl gives the man the illusion that youth is still his."

As discussed in chapter 2, most fathers of fathers' daughters lack a close relationship with their wives, and they rely on their daughters to carry their feelings and needs for them. When their daughters leave them, they not only lose a warm, ongoing relationship with the primary woman in their lives, but they are also cut off from the nurturing feelings and creative energy that infused their relationship. Diane Elizabeth Dreher analyzed the father-daughter relationship in Shakespeare's plays and noted that the fathers, who had failed to integrate their own feminine qualities, had projected these qualities onto their daughters. "When frustrated in marriage, fathers project these needs with remarkable frequency on their daughters," Dreher writes, "looking to them for beauty, purity and maternal care. Shakespeare's fathers love with a compulsiveness that approaches incest. Autocratic and possessive, they cherish their daughters and fear to lose them, for they made them the basis of their security."[4]

Many fathers become threatened as their favorite daughters develop attachments to their careers or other men; instead of striving to preserve their daughters' love in the face of these changes, they become possessive, domineering, and defiant. Dreher categorizes Shakespeare's fathers as reactionary, mercenary, egocentric, and jealous,[5] and these categories are relevant for contemporary fathers of fathers' daughters as well. A *reactionary father* refuses to acknowledge that his daughter has grown up. He does not want to give up his power in her life; he views her love for another as a blow to his pride and her new-found independence as disobedience.[6] A *mercenary father* treats his daughter as an object to be manipulated (in Shakespeare's day, sold or traded) to his advantage. In contemporary terms, the mercenary father is the narcissist who uses financial support to keep his daughter attached and therefore fulfills *his* needs. An *egocentric* father refuses to see his daughter as a separate individual and is unwilling to relinquish her. Because he perceives her as an extension of himself, with no boundaries between them, he is emotionally invasive and controlling. He cannot imagine that she would pick a spouse or career that he might disapprove of. A *jealous father* acts like a rejected lover when his daughter begins to develop a life of her own. He refuses to approve any independent choices she makes that affect his access to her. When she enters into a serious relationship with another man, he punishes her by detaching emotionally.

Most fathers' daughters have been raised to depend upon their fathers to the exclusion of all other men. The mixed messages fathers give daughters about moving beyond them inhibit their daughters' autonomy as well as make their daughters fearful of seeking emotional support from anyone else.

GO WHERE YOU WANT TO GO—BUT NEVER LEAVE ME

Many women whose fathers encouraged their independence and creativity in childhood are shocked to encounter outright resistance and disapproval when, as young women, they seek to manifest the very qualities their fathers fostered. The disapproval may take any one of the specific forms described by

Dreher in her analysis of Shakespeare's fathers. For example, writer Shirley Abbott experienced her father as a jealous, rejecting lover when she left home to pursue her writing career in New York. Abbott had been awarded an internship as a guest editor at *Mademoiselle* magazine at the end of her senior year in college. After completing the internship, she returned home to Hot Springs, Arkansas, to say good-bye to her parents before returning to live in New York. Abbott's father refused to give her his blessing and shamed her for abandoning him and her mother. They all drove to the train station in silence, her father acting as if she were a traitor, despite the fact that he had raised her to become the kind of "bookmaker" he never would be. When they arrived at the station, her father told her that she had always been a spoiled child and would be sorry when her parents were dead and gone, because no one would ever value her as much as they did. Abbott's mother tried to intervene, telling her husband to be quiet and give their daughter a chance. But her father persisted. In *The Bookmaker's Daughter*, Abbott writes:

> My father's face suddenly flooded with tears, and he took my hands in his. "You mustn't do this to me, my darling. You mustn't leave me. You're all I've got. Who will I talk to now?" "Stop, Daddy, don't." I put my arms around him. I felt deep sorrow for my mother. He could talk to her, if only he would ever try.[7]

But he never did. Abbott's father had poured all of his intellectual curiosity, repressed emotions, and unconscious hopes into his daughter, seducing her with his world of books and ideas. Now she was leaving him to participate in that world *on her own*, and he steadfastly refused to let her go. He, like many fathers of fathers' daughters, viewed her as a traitor for leaving him behind. Abbott writes:

> My father had forbidden me to go to New York, but so what? I was gone. I could live without my father's approval, maybe. The old pantheon had fallen down. If I broke Athena's bargain, as my

father construed it, to love him and serve him forever, I at least had a chance to make good on the larger contract—to become some sort of bookmaker myself. And to stand on my feet and depend on no man, another segment of the bargain I made with him, for better or for worse.[8]

Nothing Abbott did pleased her father. She worked for a year in New York in a low-level publishing job, won a graduate fellowship to study in France and then at Columbia University, became a junior editor at *Horizon* magazine, and eventually got married. Her father, too ill to attend her wedding, declared that now she was lost to him forever. He made no attempt to get acquainted, even at a distance, with her husband. He continued to diminish her professional successes and to beg her to return home.[9]

Abbott's father was blatant in his refusal to let his daughter live her own life. Not all fathers are as direct or obvious in their protestations. Another father may merely absent himself from his daughter's graduation, be too busy to read her novel, ignore her promotion, forget the day of her opening, criticize her salary, or become incapacitated on the day of her wedding. But whatever the style of communication, the rejection is always raw and painful for the daughter.

The day my agent sold this book, I phoned my father. I wanted him to be the first to know that I had contracted to write a book on the father-daughter relationship. I thought he would be thrilled with the size of my advance. Clearly, he wasn't. "Who would ever read that?" he said. When I answered that it would be of interest to both women and their fathers, as well as to new fathers raising daughters, he replied, "Well, today, I read a *real* book. On the Colt." "On the *Colt*?" I asked, confused and hurt. "You mean the horse?" "No," he replied, "The gun. You know how much I like old guns."

I was stunned, uncomprehending. I felt as if he were speaking a foreign language. Completely disillusioned, I realized that my accomplishments did not matter to my father unless they reflected his interests in some way. He has always loved finely crafted objects: maps, boats, houses, guns. My study of human relationships has never engaged him, and the fact that a major publisher wanted to publish my book had no impact on him whatsoever.

Every father's daughter wants and needs her father's approval, but if that approval is withheld she, like Abbott, will have to take the first step without him. Initially, in the chill of the severed bond, the daughter feels rejected and extremely insecure. Doubting her choices, she is beset with guilt, fearing that what she has done is wrong. She feels selfish making choices for herself: continuing school, expressing her creativity, beginning her career, spending time with friends, moving away from home. She faces the loss of her father's love if she is too assertive or too ambitious, or if she wants something for herself he doesn't want. He experiences his daughter's autonomy as a sign of rebellion and disloyalty, or at least as an affront to his life-style. At some point the daughter realizes that his price for her devotion is too high; she will never win his approval on her own terms. Loss of attachment may be her price for autonomy.

YOU'RE NOT LIKE OTHER WOMEN — YOU'RE LIKE ME

A father's daughter's prolonged dependence upon her father may resolve around another message she receives from him: *You're not like other women; you're like me.* With this message she experiences a confusing double bind: *You're not like other women* implies that other women are somehow weak and inferior and the daughter is not; *you're like me* overtly suggests that she is strong, independent, and gifted. At the same time, the covert message is, "You will do everything like I would"—definitely an insidious, limiting message.

Throughout her childhood, a father's daughter internalizes this pervasive but confusing message. Made to feel that she is the most special person in the entire world, she readily identifies with her father's thinking and actions and secretly feels that she and her father are superior to her mother and all others. As discussed in chapter 1, the daughter becomes male-favoring, valuing male intelligence and opinions and devaluing her mother and women in general. Many fathers' daughters have few women friends.

Marianne admits, "I absorbed my father's view of my mother. I started to view all women like her. He called her incompetent and mocked her. I identified with him, the victimizer, not with my mother, the victim. I didn't get actively involved in the women's movement until I healed my relationship with my mother. It has been an uphill struggle for me to identify with women, to find sisterhood, to carve out time for relationships, and to make women important in my life. Men have always been more important; women are secondary."

A father's daughter is groomed to be like her father *("You're like me")*, yet she must be sure to remain less powerful. The unspoken agreement is that she will remain loyal to him, which means upholding his values and standards. As a result, she does not develop an identity as a strong female who enjoys being a woman. The covenant with her father prevents her from forming deep relationships with either men or women or from achieving true autonomy. She may find herself in conflict every time she must choose between her father's opinions (or those of a father substitute, such as a boss, partner, or institution) and her own wishes. Her sense of loyalty to her father prevents her from standing separate and speaking *her* truth.

Waiting to Be Rescued

Most women would go to great lengths to refute the suggestion that they want to be rescued, but deep down inside, most of us *would* like to be taken care of—in a way that does not jeopardize our independence. Fathers' daughters are particularly susceptible to this dynamic. Implied in the covenant a father's daughter makes with her father is the promise that she deserves the best care available and he will always be there to provide it. But along with this reassurance of endless security, the daughter absorbs a more covert message that she is helpless and therefore needs rescuing. In addition, the father communicates in many subtle ways what type of helplessness is acceptable.

One father's daughter might learn to curtail her own growth impulses out of fear that any attempt to be independent will threaten her father. She may believe that if he is no longer allowed to play a central role in her life, he will abandon her emotionally. Another father's daughter may be encouraged to imitate her father's autonomy and outer toughness, while inwardly feeling quite insecure. Emulating her father's independent exterior but unconsciously waiting for someone to provide for her, she sabotages her own efforts to become independent.

In both situations the daughter is asked to embody the quality her father prefers—helplessness or strength. In actuality, both daughters receive the message that they are helpless, but in different ways. One is expected to show a certain degree of helplessness in designated areas, such as finances, household repairs or career decisions; the other is expected to demonstrate supreme confidence and strength yet to require her father's input on everything. Both are expected to defer to the father when *he* wants to rescue. One woman described to me how her father insisted on rescuing her whenever he had the skills—for example, in building a bookcase or having her car fixed. But when she experienced emotional difficulties and truly needed help, he lacked the skills to comfort her and instead reacted with anger and blame. The rescuing is therefore highly contingent and has less to do with what the daughter needs to become independent than with what her father needs to remain an integral part of her life.

In *The Cinderella Complex*, author Collette Dowling writes, "Here, without warning, is the truth I spend so much energy avoiding. I hate being alone. I'd like to live, marsupialized, within the skin of another. More than air and energy and life itself, what I want is to be safe, warm, taken care of."[10] Whether intended or not, Dowling here describes the extreme enmeshment that typifies a father's daughter's connection with her father. Most strong women, including feminists who pride themselves on being independent, have difficulty acknowledging the part of themselves that wants to be "marsupialized"—totally taken care of. The exception is Gloria Steinem. In her best-selling book, *Revolution from Within*, Steinem courageously admits to a period in her late forties when, exhausted from her involvement in the women's movement, she reverted to a primordial skill she hadn't used since the rise of feminism to get a man to take care of her. In this case, she chose a man with whom she had little in common. She writes: "Unlike other men in my life, who were as interested in my work as I was in theirs, and who took as much pleasure in finding books, articles, or movies that I might like as I did in doing the same for them, this man answered questions about his own life and childhood, but didn't know how to ask them of someone else."[11]

What he did know, however, was how to make her life comfortable, and Steinem, depleted by professional burnout and loss of hope, allowed herself to be provided for in a way that she had never experienced with her absent father.

"When I arrived at the airport late one night to find that he sent a car, its sheltering presence loomed out of all proportion. Remember the scene in *Bus Stop* when Marilyn Monroe, a desperate singer in a poor cafe, wraps herself in the warm, rescuing sheepskin jacket of her cowboy lover? Well, that was the way I felt sinking into that car."[12]

I think most women can relate to this desire to be rescued; I certainly can. Last year my taxes exceeded what I had estimated in my quarterly payments, and, confronted with the shock of having to liquidate my savings of the past fifteen years, I fell into the rescue-me mode. I wanted my husband or my father to sweep in and bail me out. I was angry that I had to take care of myself, yet I was also embarrassed that I wanted someone else to do it for me. In the end, I took care of myself and paid my taxes. At first, I didn't feel ennobled by the experience at all. But upon reflection, I did become conscious of how deeply this pattern of dependence and yearning is rooted in my desire to be continually provided for by a father figure, as well as my unconscious longing to remain an archetypal daughter.

Part of a woman's desire to be rescued is embedded in the fantasies reflected in fairy tales such as "Cinderella" and "Sleeping Beauty," in which the prince saves the heroine from drudgery and peril and provides her with royal status. A deeper part of the desire to be rescued is embedded in a female psychology that transfers power and responsibility to the father and other men in exchange for comfort and security. Filmmaker Gretchen, whom we met in chapter 6, says: "I was secretly waiting for some man to come along and provide me with the stuff of life. I looked at men as being like the de'Medicis. They would sweep me off my feet and take care of me. My greatest fear was that, if I had to do it myself, it wouldn't be as much fun. The fun was getting gifts, getting something from anything that's patriarchal—a father, a lover, a corporation."

Dramatic rescue fantasies emerge unbidden from within every woman. A father's daughter is even more susceptible to these romantic fantasies as a result of the particular dynamic in the father-daughter-mother triangle. Because the daughter was not nurtured by her mother in childhood, or because she herself rejected her mother, all of the daughter's fantasies about love and nurture are projected onto her father. He is the "good" parent who loves and provides for her; she is the adoring daughter who needs him and depends upon him. This early pattern has dramatic consequences later in life when she enters adult relationships with men. Although she may view herself as a liberated, responsible woman, she may unconsciously expect her spouse to provide for her. For example, a daughter whose father did not teach her financial responsibility may learn the art of manipulation to get what she wants. If she is able to cajole her father into buying her a new toy, Rollerblades, designer jeans, and later a car, she learns that coyness and persuasion are powerful tools. As an adult, she continues to practice the art of manipulation in all her relationships. She may tell herself that she is functioning as a fully independent adult, but unconsciously she does not want to take *full* responsibility for her share. Whether it is a lunch bill, rent check, tax payment, tuition, household expense, or entertainment expense, she would like someone else to pick up the tab.

If a woman's relationship with men, starting in early childhood with her father, has been based on dependency and need, how can she free herself from this type of relationship? Only by becoming conscious of how she is replicating the conditions of her relationship with her father and acknowledging the deleterious consequences for her adult relationships. This emerging awareness is usually preceded by feelings of deprivation and rage, and attempts at manipulation—the daughter's "last stand" before accepting responsibility to make her life work.

Turning the Corner: Developing Autonomy as a Woman

Because a father's daughter has identified so closely with her father, she is faced with a greater challenge than other daughters to individuate from him and, at the same time, maintain an emotional connection. Separation from the father begins when the young adult discovers and expresses the ingredients of her identity—her needs, beliefs, values, goals, and talents—that are separate from his. In this process, she also becomes aware of how her identification with her father has served her in many positive ways. In many cases, the father has been a bridge across the currents of the outer world and, as a result, she has become comfortable navigating them. Because he has endowed her with a sense of how special she is to him, she never expects to be treated differently as a woman. But as she examines other ramifications of their relationship, dissonant aspects surface. For example, finally disagreeing with her father on issues that are important to her, she is stunned and angered when he dismisses or rejects her independent point of view. Weaving the fabric of her own identity, she may discover many feelings and opinions that have deadened in an effort to reflect his. Recognizing this implicit contradiction of apparent autonomy and stifling dependence is the first step toward her independent identity.

Fortunate is the daughter whose father actively fosters her emotional and financial autonomy as she grows into a young woman.

From the time she was very small, Pat, the physician whom we met in chapter 2, expected to support herself. Her father provided well for the family but never demanded a dependent relationship. He treated each family member as an equal, and sons and daughters alike were encouraged to fulfill their potential. Pat also observed him dealing with his employees equitably regardless of race or gender. She expected the same treatment when she entered the medical world.

When she finished her specialty in anesthesiology in the early fifties, her boss at the hospital informed her that she would not receive the same salary as the male doctors because they had families to support. Pat protested this position as unfair; doctors are paid for the work they do, not the number of people they have to support. She told her superior that she should get paid the same salary for the same day's work.

She says, "My dad had always talked about the fact that you reimburse people for what they do, regardless of race or gender. His attitude was, an honest day's pay for an honest day's work. He never differentiated. So it seemed perfectly reasonable to me to ask for what I was worth." Because Pat's father had imparted to her an expectation of equality, she naturally valued her medical skills as being equal to those of her male colleagues and was therefore firm in her demand to receive the same salary. Her demand was met.

Cutting the Purse Strings While Leaving the Heartstrings Intact

Most fathers' daughters find that they have to initiate their own efforts to carve out an emotional and financial autonomy. Tamar, whom we met in chapter 6, had to struggle for her autonomy, first by being willing to let go of her father's financial assistance, and then by making her own decisions.

"My father never encouraged me to make decisions on my own," she says. "Autonomy is something I've had to fight for. Once I figured out how to get it, I said to him, 'These are the new rules,' and he said, 'Okay.' But having his daughter function as an independent adult certainly wasn't his idea. And it wasn't easy for me either. He was giving me money to supplement my income, and when I finally mustered the courage to ask him to stop, I wondered if I really meant it!"

Tamar's father made decisions for everyone in the family. As an engineer, he seemed to have a solution for every problem. Tamar recalled, "If I said, 'Dad, I'm going to do X,' he'd say, 'Why don't you do it this way?' I learned to bring him the problem and he'd tell me what to do. He meant well, but meanwhile I never learned to think things through on my own."

When she went to work as a young adult, Tamar realized she needed to operate differently. Her boss naturally expected her to solve problems on her own, and she soon discovered that she could.

"I never took that first step with my father and said, 'Don't

help me; I want to do this myself,' Tamar continues. "I had to face that I wasn't making decisions for myself even though I had the capability to do so. Now when I say, 'I'm going to do X,' and he says, 'Why don't you do it this way?' I say, 'Because I've thought it through and I don't want to do it that way.' I don't ask him what to do anymore. It's a mixed blessing; he's glad that I'm thinking for myself, but I know he also wants to be needed. But he doesn't complain."

Wedding Bells: Staying Connected While Giving One's Heart to Another

The separation process between father and daughter intensifies when the father's daughter decides to marry. Whether the marriage ruptures their bond or brings a new closeness depends upon the willingness of both to grow beyond their habitual patterns of interaction.

Chelsea observed, to her displeasure, that her father's desire for control initially increased when she become engaged. He was adamant about giving her and her fiance, Jim, an engagement party that neither of them wanted. She knew that it was important to her father to have the party; he wanted his friends to admire his daughter and meet his future son-in-law. She decided that it was not worth the fight. What was really important to her was the spiritual aspect of the wedding ceremony. Her father wanted a friend of his to perform the ceremony, but she told him no. She and Jim picked a rabbi they admired to officiate.

Chelsea and Jim took her mother and father out for drinks on the latter's sixty-fifth birthday. When the bill came, Jim paid for it in spite of her father's protests. Chelsea explained to her father that it was time for him to allow them to give to him; that their desire to pay the bill was not about control but about love. She says, "After he got used to the idea, he really liked it. If it were up to him, nothing would change. He'd be one hundred years old and still paying for everything. But something changed that night. He understood that it was okay to receive. Something softened in him. I feel like I have some authority now and I don't have to act like a rebellious child or adolescent to get what I want from him."

Chelsea worked successfully to separate from her father yet remain emotionally connected. For a daughter to take this step toward autonomy yet remain close with her father, she must engage him in the process and he must be willing to participate. In the following example, the father remains emotionally connected to his daughter as long as he can function as provider.

Marty's early marriage at the age of twenty-one abruptly ended the intimacy she had always shared with her father, as well as her feelings of being special. She and her husband moved away to another city, and contact with her father waned. He said he didn't want to interfere with her marriage, but she sensed that her father viewed her husband as having displaced the central position he had occupied in her life. She experienced tremendous loss as a result of his emotional withdrawal.

Eleven years later, her marriage ended in divorce and her relationship with her father changed. Not knowing how to relate to her as a single adult woman, Marty's father communicated with her through the one role with which he was familiar, and which she now shared: as one head-of-household to another, discussing finances, business, and maintenance of the house. He felt that it was important for her children to have as little disruption as possible during and after the divorce; so they wouldn't have to move, he contributed to her mortgage payments for three years until she could pay the full amount. Marty never could have managed the mortgage on her salary alone; his assistance ensured her family's stability. Her divorced status had bestowed on her an odd kind of respect and financial power—as seen through her father's eyes.

Marty's second marriage five years later brought her emotional connection to her father abruptly to an end. He said simply that now she "belonged" to another. Deprived of her reliance on him, Marty's father again withdrew from their relationship. Now she rarely hears from him. Their relationship remained intact only when her father felt needed and another man was absent; the presence of her husband precluded intimacy with her.

Many fathers of adult daughters find it difficult to relate to competent, independent women who need neither their emotional nor financial support. Men are used to solving problems and giving counsel; they are at a loss with daughters who want neither their solutions nor advice. Men in their sixties, seventies, and eighties today have limited experience in relating to women as peers. They therefore treat their daughters as invisible, as caretakers, as sons, or like rejecting lovers.

It takes courage for a daughter to say no to her father, make her own choices, and seek her own approval and validation. But if a daughter is to separate her identity from her father's and release her own energy, at some point she must reject his external authority and become self-reliant. In the process, painful though it is at times, she develops a capacity for self-reflection, deliberation, and initiative that eventually breaks the underlying threads of the bond that has bound her to him.

A daughter may have success in initiating a change in her relationship with her father by letting him know who *she* is. In most cases, the father has taught his daughter about the outer world. As he ages and she becomes knowledgeable about areas with which he has no contact, their roles may reverse. In later years, many men take an interest in communicating with their daughters about their personal past, family history, the natural world, and spiritual concerns. Most daughters already have the tools to enter these arenas. It may be here that father and daughter can find common ground and begin to create space for deeper mutual love and understanding.

Jump and I'll Catch You:
Separation Through Betrayal

Many fathers' daughters do not separate psychologically from their fathers until an unexpected variable intervenes: marriage, betrayal, illness, or death. We have already seen how marriage can catalyze separation; here, we will look at the positive and negative consequences of what is experienced as *betrayal*. The covenant between a father's daughter and her father ensures that he will protect her. Her identity, enmeshed with his, is predicated on the trust embedded in this contract, and her trust in her father depends upon his ability to keep his part of the agreement to protect and provide for her. If her father fails to protect her, she becomes confused and disillusioned. She cannot understand his failure as anything less than a betrayal because, from her point of view, she has upheld her part of the covenant to be loyal to him.

When there is no special bond between father and daughter and the daughter is left unprotected, she certainly experiences hurt and disappointment, but her expectations are not as unrealistic, and therefore the sense of betrayal is not as strong. A father's daughter is often devastated by her father's inability to keep the promise embedded in her very identity: "You are the most special person in the world, and I will do anything for you as long as you also will do anything for me." The father's daughter feels that she has done everything for her father, and she is shaken when he lets her down. Her eventual disillusionment with the covenant may ultimately release her to individuate from him. The following story (adapted from a story about a father and his son) illustrates how a father's deliberate betrayal actually helps his daughter learn to rely upon herself.

A father was teaching his little daughter to be less afraid, to have more courage, by having her jump down the stairs outside their apartment. He placed her on the second stair and said, "Jump and I'll catch you." And the little girl jumped, and her father

191

caught her. Then the father placed her on the third stair and said, "Jump and I'll catch you." The little girl was afraid, but she was a good girl who trusted her father, and so she did what her father told her to do. She jumped right into his arms. Then her father placed her on the next stair, and the next, and so on, each time telling her, "Jump and I'll catch you." And each time, she jumped and he caught her. When she reached the top stair, she jumped just as she had before, but this time the father stepped back and did not catch her. The little girl fell flat on her face. She picked herself up, bleeding and crying, and the father said to her, "Never trust anyone, even if it's your own father."[13]

This is a story about betrayal and trust, which are two sides of the same coin. You cannot have betrayal without trust, nor trust without the possibility of betrayal.[14] A child cannot stay in a stage of eternal trust with her father for the simple reason that, sooner or later, he is bound to break a promise, disappoint her, or, like the father in the tale "The Handless Maiden," fail to keep the world at bay. He wouldn't be human if he didn't. Nonetheless, a daughter whose very identity is symbolically entwined with her father's will feel an enormous shock when he fails her. How she copes with this shock will determine whether or not she successfully separates from him.

Analyzing this story, Archetypal analyst James Hillman writes, "If one leaps where there are always arms to take one up, there is no real leap."[15] How true this is, and how difficult the lesson: A father's daughter must move beyond the security of her father's arms in order to have her own life. She has to leave the known—the familiar territory of their covenant—and take back her projections about him. Sometimes this leave-taking is triggered by a betrayal of her trust. The betrayal marks the death of her innocence and the birth of her consciousness—if she chooses to understand its full meaning.

Connie, the minister's daughter whom we met in chapter 7, grew up with a mother who was emotionally and physically abusive. While Connie was a little girl, her two older sisters acted as a buffer, but when they left home, she became the sole focus of her mother's frustration and anger. At the age of fifteen, Connie went to her father with a list of suggestions about how he could protect her from her mother. She pleaded with him to do one of the following: get a divorce, send her away to boarding school, let her live with an older sister, or arrange family counseling for the three of them. He said no to each suggestion. It wouldn't look right for a minister to divorce his wife or to send his daughter away. If they went for family counseling, everyone would know that something was wrong with the family. Connie walked out of his office feeling disappointed, sickened, and utterly abandoned. From that moment on, as she put it, "I cut him out of my heart." In therapy twenty-eight years later, Connie realized that she had never again been emotionally available to her father, because of his refusal to protect her. She also admitted that she had never taken responsibility for her detachment, blaming it on him. Now she acknowledged, "Whatever I missed out on was as much my choice as it was his."

It is very common for a daughter to blame her father, or her mother or siblings, for what she did not receive from her father. Blame, however, keeps a woman an archetypal daughter, forever waiting to be rescued. If she refuses to look at her father from an adult perspective, understanding his limitations as a man as well as the social limitations of the time, she remains emotionally tied to him in a childlike state. She continues to resent him as the all-powerful parent who withheld his support, instead of understanding and accepting his failings as a human being.

Connie began to accept her father's limitations and took responsibility for her part in restricting their relationship. She realized that her father was unable to stand up to his wife's tyranny. He did not know how to stop her abuse and, as the minister in a small Texas town, was too ashamed to seek help. Once she realized this, Connie was able to mourn for the child who was not protected by her father, understand his wounds, and finally separate his wounds from hers. This does not mean that she absolved him of his responsibility to have protected her as a child, only that she understood the dysfunctionality of the entire family system. She was then able to establish new emotional connections with him as an adult, with no expectations of his being her savior.

Until a father's daughter becomes conscious of her enmeshment with her father, she, like Connie, will use her father's betrayal or failures to deny his value as a person and view him *only* as a perpetrator of her hurt. She will remain entrenched in the belief that he failed to protect her, provide for her, back her up; that he alienated her affections, betrayed a secret, kicked her out of the nest, let the world intervene. Embittered by his betrayal, the daughter rejects her father, refuses his phone calls, moves to another city. Unable to forgive him, she carries the trauma into other relationships. She may decide that no man is trustworthy and shut herself off from the possibility of a man's love. Or she may punish every man that follows in her father's footsteps, continually disappointed when each fails, inevitably, to meet her expectations. Since her father failed her, she has even higher expectations for her spouse: He must not only rescue her but also make up for the wounds of the father.

Hillman asks us to look at the betrayal in "Jump and I'll Catch You" within a wider context of love and necessity—that the father risks his daughter's broken bones, broken trust, and broken image of him to help her move beyond him.[16] The father, of course, must then live with his guilt and pain, particularly if his daughter refuses to forgive him. But this view implies that the father's act is a *conscious* one of love and sacrifice. How many fathers consciously betray a child's trust out of a desire to promote his or her autonomy? Not many. In real life, it is usually a father's human limitations and weaknesses that inadvertently coalesce into the betrayal.

If the daughter is able to view the betrayal as an opportunity for growth, however, she will brush herself off, look for meaning, and move beyond blaming her father. Recognizing that her father is fallible and has limitations, she will give up her childlike expectations and simultaneously gain her selfhood. This is not done without pain. Remembering and forgiving are part of making both daughter and father conscious of the meaning of the betrayal. Forgiving becomes possible only when the betrayal is viewed within the larger context of the entire father-daughter relationship. On one hand, the father's betrayal of the daughter appears to be his sin, yet some form of betrayal from one side or the other is required if the daughter is ever to become her own person. The adult father's daughter needs to admit this in order to see her father as a human being. It may take years for the betrayal to be understood and years for forgiveness to occur. For the final integration of both the positive and negative aspects of the experience to take place, there must be a reconciliation by both daughter and father, perhaps not to each other but to the circumstances of the event.[17]

If a father has died or remains emotionally unavailable, the daughter needs support to express her anger and loss. Until the pain of the wounding is expressed, she will remain tied to her father in disappointment, anger, and regret. She needs to be heard by a friend, a therapist, a support group. Giving expression in art or writing is another form of healing. She must have the opportunity to move forward. Social philosopher Madonna Kolbenschlag writes, "There are points in life when the soul/self must either expand or contract. Consciousness cannot remain neutral. A decision must be made, consequences accepted. We are never the same afterward."[18]

Separation Through Illness

A father's illness is often a turning point in the father-daughter relationship. As he ages, a father may be faced with deteriorating health, the inevitability of dependence upon his daughter, and a dramatic exchange of roles. The daughter becomes caretaker to a man who bears little resemblance to the father of her youth. His once formidable presence and dominance are muted by declining health. Father and daughter adjust to changing perceptions of each other; as he becomes vulnerable, childlike, and dependent upon her, it may be the first time he accepts her as an adult.

Marianne's father turned sixty-eight this year and had quadruple bypass surgery. He is the only male in his family that has survived early heart attacks. As Marianne fed him during his recovery, she realized that it was the first time she had ever experienced her father's vulnerability. She says, "He has been totally in charge my whole life. I feel incredibly sad. I feel like I'm losing him. Part of me likes less dominance, but losing control is different from letting go of control. Watching him age is frightening; I'm looking at my own mortality."

A father's illness may affect siblings in very different ways, depending on the nature of their relationships and the degree to which they have been able to individuate. Phoebe and Alice have very different relationships with their father: Phoebe is the father's daughter, and Alice is "the baby" in her father's eyes. The sisters share a warm, loving relationship with each other as well as a wonderful sense of humor. Though in their forties, neither has ever married and each, in her own way, is devoted to their father. After their mother died, he developed Alzheimer's disease, and they have shared the burden of caring for him. For ten years, Alice, a schoolteacher, took care of him at home on a daily basis, and Phoebe relieved her sister during holidays and summer vacations from her university teaching position in another state. They recently decided, along with their two brothers, to put him in a nursing home.

Phoebe was always her father's favorite, and he gave her considerable responsibility and attention as she was growing up. He treated her like a son, teaching her how to wire lamps, change fuses, and fix things around the house. He sought her out on Friday nights when he came home from drinking with his buddies. Knowing that she had a calming influence on her father, Phoebe would sit up with him half the night, making coffee and listen to his philosophizing. Phoebe was the first child in the family to go out of state for college; after completing graduate studies in biology, she went into cancer research. Alice, in contrast, stayed at home, attended a local college, and subsequently taught in the local junior high. As "the baby" in this New England Irish-Catholic family, Alice was given only limited responsibility, and the type of attention she received from her father was for being a "small, cute thing." In his eyes, she never grew up, and his idealization of her as a child made it difficult for her to function like an adult.

Their father's deteriorating health has forced both sisters to confront their own issues about letting him go. This has been easier for Phoebe because her father affirmed her status and power as a child and treats her like an adult today. She says, "He had a theory that there was one person who would keep the family together and that would be me. He told me to make sure we would all be close. I had a vision of myself as the world's youngest martyr, listening to his alcoholic ramblings, and I certainly got the message that I had to cure the world's ills." Her father encouraged her to be the best that she could be, and she lived up to his image of her. She received her doctorate, became a radiation biologist, and achieved the position of first woman chairperson of her faculty in the 125-year history of her college. Phoebe feels complete with her father; she has no missing pieces.

In contrast, Alice never received recognition of her worth and abilities from her father, and he refused to accept her as a competent adult even when he was faced with physical dependence upon her. In fact, he repeatedly called Phoebe to tell her that Alice was stealing his money and trying to poison him by cooking him "road kills." Alice's greatest challenge has been combatting her father's demeaning image of her as a child and confronting the fact that they have never had a mature relationship. In fact, they had almost no relationship whatsoever until his mental faculties deteriorated and he became dependent on her.

"Our relationship really developed when he started to become senile and I started standing up for myself," Alice says. "I would scream, 'Dad, I can do this. You've got to trust me because I'm the only one here.' He's more comfortable now; I've taken good care of him, and I've finally started to feel good about that. But I don't know if I did it for my father, as I knew him, or the man he has become. The man I have taken care of is definitely not my father. He is like a child; we have changed roles."

What is poignant about the stories of these two sisters is the differing impact the father had on each daughter's self-esteem. The father saw Phoebe as a highly competent individual who would achieve great things; she left home and carried forth his destiny. He never gave Alice any encouragement and viewed her as an eternal child; she never left home. Her father's respect helped Phoebe to separate from him, and she has no regrets about their relationship. For Alice, it was only after her father became incapacitated that she was able to feel like a competent adult and begin to differentiate herself from his narrow, limiting view. She is still struggling with the fact that her father never validated her. She says:

"I took over for Phoebe, but I didn't become Phoebe in his eyes. He realizes that he was dependent on me and so he finally stopped reacting to me as if I were a child. But I'm definitely not a full-grown, forty-four-year-old woman to him. And I don't believe that I behave that way when I'm with him. I think I'm stuck in that image of myself, too."

Alice is beginning to reclaim her life. After her father went into the nursing home, she couldn't visit him for the first three months.

"I went through a mourning period," she says. "It angers me that, even though I willingly chose to care for him, I was also goaded into doing it by family beliefs about the youngest's duties. I bought into those beliefs; I arranged my life, forsaking other pathways, so that I could live at home. This past year has been a freeing experience, but I'm still cocooning rather than spreading my wings."

What is unusual in this example is that the two sisters are like twin vessels, each carrying some qualities embodied by fathers' daughters. The oldest daughter, Phoebe, idealized by her father to be a competent, responsible adult, has been able to separate from him by virtue of the roles he bestowed upon her. He gave her leave to fulfill his projected image of her as a successful career woman; at the same time, he entrusted her with the role of keeping the family connected. In the case of Alice, her father selfishly kept her for himself by virtue of his dependency upon her, which he never openly admitted. Despite the fact that Alice cared for his health, home, and finances while holding a full-time teaching job, he never acknowledged her competency until his debilitation forced him to accept it. Phoebe's individuation from her father remains partial because it is, in some ways, a living-out of his projections; but Alice has had to enact the full struggle of individuation from her father by giving up her "special" role as baby, and proving her adult status by ending the dependent relationship he fostered.

Death and Letting Go

The loss of a beloved father is never easy for his daughter, but if she has been able to establish a mature relationship with him, unfettered by need and dependence, and filled with mutual respect, she will have an easier time dealing with his inevitable death. If a father dies when his daughter is still a child, and still enmeshed in her idealization of him, she will have a difficult time letting him go even as an adult. As we will see, both the timing and the manner of a father's death greatly affect his daughter's response to her loss.

Kris's father died when she was thirteen. Like other daughters whose relationships with their fathers are severed through death when they are young, Kris continues to idealize him. Growing up in the Midwest, her movie-handsome father came into her bedroom at night and sat on her bed to talk. He wanted to hear everything about her day. He was a blue-collar worker in a meat packing plant, a man who had never completed his high school education. But he wanted Kris to have a life filled with culture and art. She says, "He always encouraged me to express my creativity. When I wanted to paint, he bought me paints. When I wanted to sculpt, he took me to the quarry to find stone. Whenever I was with him, I felt like 'his girl.' That was fine until I became a teenager and his possessiveness became suffocating."

Kris felt the constant tension between her father and mother and knew her father preferred her to her mother. Kris and her mother always fought and her favored status with her father only contributed to her mother's jealous rage. Her father's abrupt death left her unprotected from her mother and has had a lasting impact on her relationships with men.

"When my father died thirty years ago, I went into shock—and it still affects me to this day! I felt very guilty about my father's death. He forbade me from having a boyfriend, and the morning he died we had a terrible fight over a boy he thought was my boyfriend. When he had his accident at work, I was sure that I was responsible for his death.

I missed a natural progression from childhood to maturity; when I want intimacy with a man, I revert to acting like a thirteen-year-old. I've made some very bad choices with men; I've wanted a daddy to take care of me but a man like that thinks he can con-

trol and dominate me like a little girl. When I fall for a man who doesn't need to control me, I'm afraid he'll leave me like my father did."

Kris knows that she is still locked in a love affair with her father. Her attachment to her idealization of him and her guilt about his death prevents her from having a mature relationship with a man. She attracts men who want to take care of her and then she struggles to extricate herself from their grasp. Her present challenge is to give up the myth that she killed her father, to face the fact that he will never return to affirm her as an adult, and to individuate from him by allowing a man to love her as an equal.

The circumstances of Luella's father's death also made it impossible for her to say good-bye. Despite the fact that she was in her early thirties when her father died, Luella was still enmeshed in their relationship, and his death eventually forced her to differentiate from him. Luella's father was fatally struck by lightning during a family vacation in Georgia. The afternoon before they were to return home, her father took her out for their annual ritual lunch to discuss the state of the world and the family: her mother, her brother's marriage, his friends, the farm, and her dogs.

"We were in Sea Island and we went to a seafood restaurant," Luella remembers. *"He was drinking a beer and smoking his annual cigarette. When he was relaxing, he'd smoke a cigarette like it was his first experience with a cigarette in his mouth. It was an endearing, peculiar sight. He wore a red shirt, and he talked about everything. It was almost an award banquet for our relationship. But he seemed sadder this time; there was an overtone of disappointment that wasn't normally the case."*

Luella and her father finished lunch, got in the car, drove down a little sandy road, and looked at the water. Then they went to see a condominium complex where her father talked to the salesman about hunting and English setters—part "good ol' boy" conversation, part business discussion. The salesman assumed that Luella was her father's wife, and her father did nothing to dissuade him of his impression.

They went back to the house they were renting and parked the car, and Luella thanked her father for lunch. The sky darkened, and family members began to take things inside the house to prepare for the upcoming storm. Without saying a word, Luella's father went to the dock to bring in chairs. Luella recalls, "We were all standing there watching when the lightning struck. We heard a huge sound, followed by a big blast of circular light that hit a two-by-four pylon. It electrified the area where my father was standing. He fell backward, and then there was an enormous blast of rain. Despite efforts to revive him, his heart stopped beating within the hour."

Luella felt that her father's death was consistent with the way he had lived his life: testing, disregarding, and defying nature. "His lightning-quick death was fitting. He was classically more concerned with being active, the schedule, and the goal. There was no time for reflection or waiting. As a hunter, he was fascinated by the habits of animals he hunted, but it was more important to him to prevail over them. He was the dominator. He could feel a passing sense of wonder and appreciation, but he couldn't let go and give in to it. He was not geared to go into another phase of life as an older man who could no longer be like John Wayne. He couldn't have handled the debilitation."

Luella felt like she was going to die after her father's death. She floated around in a "netherworld" for a couple of weeks, certain that it was just a matter of days before something would happen to her. If he could die, she could die, too. A bicycle accident shook her out of the romantic notion that she would follow her father in death.

"I realized it was not my time. I told myself to get on with it,

grieve, and not get stuck in the drama of my pain. I started meditating, became more moderate, stopped working so much, rested, and accepted the awful pain of losing my champion . . . losing someone who always approved of me, who was always there to give me that squinty, knowing look that said, 'You're alright.' I thought, How could this person die? If he could die, anyone could die. My net is gone, my security is gone. This man in a man's world is gone. I don't have that protection anymore."

But Luella also realized that her father was ready to "move on." Everyone in the family was in good shape, and he didn't have any serious problems to solve. She realized that she had modeled her father's addiction to activity in her own life and that his death had helped her to slow down and break this pattern. She had become adept at playing the game of looking good, denying her low self-esteem by overworking, and using recreational drugs.

"My father's behavior gave me license for my own behavior. Working all the time, I became my father. Part of me still wants to emulate him lock, stock, and barrel, but to continue to live his life the way he lived is endangering: working maniacally, valuing activity over anything else, devaluing relationship, thinking I'm right. The best part that I can take from what he taught me is a certain resourcefulness, and that allows for both productivity and freedom. He was a strong model for that, and it works."

Luella is clear about which aspects of her father she wishes to embody and which she needs to leave behind. This discrimination is key to the individuation process. Each generation carries the father forward, and every daughter learns something from her father's life. Her choice is what to embody and what to bless and release. It is difficult to separate from the father if a daughter remains wounded by events surrounding her father's death, divorce, illness, abuse, or betrayal. She then embodies his pain rather than his value. Healing those wounds is necessary for a daughter to move on. She can then choose an emotional connection with the father who gave her value, identify with the strengths she wants to carry, and eliminate the behavior and attitudes that no longer fit.

Beauty and the Beast: *Autonomy and Emotional Connection*

Beauty and the Beast is a remarkably clear and poignant story of a daughter's individuation from her father. Because Beauty succeeds in finding love, self-knowledge, and autonomy, as well as retaining an emotional connection with her father, her story brings a fitting end to this chapter.

In the popular fairy tale written in the eighteenth century by Madame Leprince de Beaumont, a rich, widowed merchant has three fair daughters, the youngest of whom is named Beauty.[19] The father unexpectedly loses his wealth, and the family is forced to move out of the city and live in poorer circumstances. Shortly after their move, the father has to take a trip to settle his affairs, and he asks his daughters what they wish upon his return. The two elder sisters ask for beautiful gowns, but Beauty asks for nothing. When her father insists, she asks for a rose.

The father's trip is a disappointment financially, and he is forced to return home as poor as he left. He gets lost in the forest and spends the night in a strange castle where he finds food and shelter but no inhabitants. When he departs in the morning, he sees a garden of beautiful roses and remembers his young daughter's request. He picks a rose for Beauty. Instantly, a horrible Beast appears and berates him for stealing the flower. He tells the merchant he will have to die. The merchant explains that he took the rose for his daughter, Beauty, and the Beast tells him that he will spare his life if one of his daughters will take his place. He gives the merchant three months to put his affairs in order and bid farewell to his family. He then sends him on his way with a chest of gold.

The merchant returns home in desolation and gives Beauty the rose. The gold provides the sisters a suitable dowry. When Beauty hears her father's story, she insists on taking his place. He refuses, but she persists. After three months, Beauty accompanies her father, against his will, to the castle. The Beast asks Beauty if she has come of her own free will, and she says yes. Beauty and her father have a tearful parting, and the Beast sends her father home.

In the castle, Beauty has all of her needs met, yet she is very lonely. She longs for her family. Each night the Beast visits her during dinner, and each night he asks her to become his wife. Each night she refuses. Over the next three months, Beauty and Beast spend more time together, reading and enjoying each other's company. The Beast continues to ask her to be his bride, and she gently refuses. He then asks Beauty to never leave him. She promises this much but asks to visit her father, whom she knows is ill and longing for her. The Beast has a magical mirror through which she can see her father's weakening condition. The Beast gives her a week to visit her family, warning her that he will die if she does not return within that time.

The next morning Beauty finds herself at home with her father, who is overjoyed to see her. She is so happy to be with him and her sisters that she extends her visit beyond the week. On the tenth night, Beauty dreams that the Beast is dying of a broken heart because she has failed to keep her promise. She then realizes how deeply attached she has become to the Beast and immediately returns to him. Finding him near death, Beauty tells the Beast that she loves him and that she wishes to marry him. At this, the Beast turns into a prince. An evil spell has been broken. Beauty's father returns with the rest of the family to witness the marriage.

Beauty is so named because of the purity of her nature. She lives in harmony with both her inner life and her outer surroundings. In "The Resurrection of the Body in Cocteau's *Beauty and the Beast*," Larry Gates writes, "everyone lives a myth, and Beauty's myth at the beginning of the story is that she is her father's girl. The two of them enjoy a special relationship that is pristine, platonic and virtuous. Since there is no mother in the family, Beauty has Daddy all to herself."[20]

Beauty's life with her father is peaceful, but it is time for her to move beyond the stage of innocence and childhood. She has never left the security of the family circle. In choosing to sacrifice her life for her father's, she begins a journey of individuation. In the presence of the Beast, Beauty awakens to her own physical and sensual nature and embarks on an inner journey of self-examination and awareness. The Beast's compassion and loving nature overshadow his monstrous appearance. When Beauty decides to leave her father and willingly marry the Beast, she grows from daughter to adult.

Beauty's love restores the Beast's human nature. She loses the Beast for the prince, but the Beast has awakened her instinctual and sensual nature and becomes part of her inner landscape.[21] In making a conscious choice to love, Beauty accepts responsibility for both her inner and outer lives. Separating from her father, she achieves personal autonomy. A father's daughter can have a mature, intimate relationship with a lover only when both daughter and father are willing to let go. In doing so, Beauty also gives her father the kind of affection most beneficial to him; she honors him as sage and elder.

The emotional separation process for a father's daughter begins when she first *recognizes* the degree of her attachment to her father, develops the *willingness* to let go of the rewards of being his special girl, and finally *takes concrete steps* to extricate herself from emotional and financial dependence. The betrayal of their covenant, by either father or daughter, ultimately helps the daughter individuate. Marriage may facilitate the necessary transfer of her primary love attachment from her father to her spouse, a father's illness may break the cycle of his daughter's dependence, and his ultimate death forces her to let go. Betrayal, marriage, illness, and death are hallmark events that catalyze the first steps of the separation process. In the final chapter, we will discuss the more subtle threads that continue to bind a father's daughter to her father and the delicate process of unravelling them.

Take My Heart by Maureen Murdock.
(Watercolor, pastel, and ink on paper, 11 × 14 in., 1994.
Reprinted by permission of the artist.)

CHAPTER NINE

Coming to Terms with Father

> I am a woman. I cannot be free while I am a daughter possessed by the *Father inside my head*. . . . To canonize my biological father at the expense of my mythic father, to absolve my physical father by projecting onto the interior father every dark thing that father means in a sexist society, will bring me no nearer to the truth—about myself, or him, or fathers, or daughters.
>
> —Sara Maitland, "Two for the Price of One"

A FATHER'S daughter is caught in a finely woven web of projections and expectations that binds her to her father. She may feel quite independent from him as she develops her career and nurtures the relationships in her life, yet part of her unconscious focus is always on her father, wondering what he would think, whether he would approve. Their bond is like an umbilical cord that has never been cut. Until the daughter is willing to examine the subtle, lingering threads that weave back and forth between her and her father, she will remain an archetypal daughter.

A father's daughter is caught in a suspended state of *yearning*, underneath which lies denial of her loss—the loss of the broken covenant. She yearns for the impossible: her father's *uncondi-*

tional love, respect, support, and recognition: his undivided interest and male presence. She yearns for his approval of *all* areas of her life: her husband or partner, her children, her work, her hard-won maturity, even her friends and her reading material. She remains identified with her father's value system or unconsciously tries to change his values to match her own. This continuous undercurrent of attachment drains her energy and keeps her in a passive, childlike state of waiting for his validation.

If a father failed to give his daughter what she yearned for as a child in one area or another—approval of her choices, recognition of her mental abilities, support for her dreams, financial security, protection, permission to be separate from him—she will project these unfulfilled cravings onto others in her adult life—lovers, friends, and bosses alike. She constantly longs for another "daddy" to make up for what her father failed to give her, and she refuses to accept that she will never get what she longed for as a child. For example, although my father nurtured my intellectual abilities, he failed to nurture the more impractical side of my nature, my fantasies and dreams. Throughout my childhood and early adulthood, I continued to give him opportunities to do so, obstinately refusing to accept his limitations in this area. His inability to support my dreams did not squelch my yearnings, however; in fact, it intensified them because I became fixated on the fantasy that a man could make my dreams come true.

One dream, in particular, wound its way into my adult life. When I was a little girl, my father promised to build me a playhouse. We talked about it year after year, and he drew plan after plan. I entered into his architectural vision of the playhouse and entertained my own dreams about how it would look, what kind of curtains I'd make for the windows, the tea parties I'd have with my dolls, what fun we'd have. It was the perfect fantasy for a father's daughter: Daddy building a miniature house just for her, separate from Mommy, where she could have him all to herself.

My father never built the playhouse; it remained nothing more than a carefully drawn architectural plan. Recently I realized how this early unmet yearning has contaminated my relationship with my husband and sabotaged my personal power. Repeatedly throughout my marriage, I tried to persuade my husband to help me buy a cabin in the country where I could retreat and write. Although I could afford the down payment myself, I persistently tried to get *him* to enter my fantasy and actualize it *for* me. (My husband says I want a "cash cow" to finance my dream!) Unconsciously, I wanted my husband to give me the "playhouse" my father failed to build. My husband's reluctance to do so unconsciously constellated my deep disappointment in my father but got acted out as a power struggle between my husband and myself. The cabin as playhouse became a symbol not only of my lost childhood dreams, but also of the protection from my mother I yearned for as a child that my father could not give.

A father's daughter's unwillingness to relinquish her yearnings, once she becomes aware of them, is partially embedded in the sense of entitlement engendered by her relationship with her father. As discussed previously, the father of a father's daughter treats his daughter as special and communicates, in one way or another, that he will do *anything* in the world for her (as long as she continues to remain loyal to him). Raised to believe that she is indeed special, the daughter feels *entitled* to get what she wants. And she won't take no for an answer.

Most fathers' daughters have learned that they can get what they *want* in an aggressive, extroverted manner, but they typically fail to get what they *yearn for*, because their yearnings are more subtle, less clearly perceived, and bear the wounds of their childhoods and their alienation from their mothers. These daughters yearn for recognition of the softer, more soulful, more feminine aspects of their psyche: the need to be mothered and comforted, the need to listen to their own instinctual natures, the need to create their own dreams and actualize their fantasies. They stumble and falter in the face of these wistful yet compelling yearnings. They have consistently relied upon their real fathers and their internalized fathering functions to guide them in the outer world, but the teachings of the father do not include knowledge about how the inner and outer worlds work *together*.[1] Unfamiliar with turning inward to listen to their own deep wisdom, fathers' daughters look outside themselves, often futilely, for the fulfillment of their yearnings.

When a woman continues to feel *entitled* to get whatever she desires, the inflated entitlement signifies that she is still bound to her father. If one man, or job, or situation fails to meet her yearnings, she will seek another, and another, expecting something that, in fact, no one can ever *give* to her. She will always be disappointed because unconsciously she is still waiting for and wanting her father to provide what he promised to give. To sever the archetypal promise that she will always be provided for and protected, a father's daughter must give up her desire that her father (or his substitute) fulfill her needs. She doesn't have to give up her dreams and wishes, but she does have to realize that to be psychologically whole, she has to learn to provide for and protect herself. Reconciling herself to this reality is a long, subtle process and, like every other aspect of psychological growth, passes through several stages: denial, rage, suffering and grief, understanding, and eventual acceptance.

Untangling the Web of Projections and Expectations

A father's daughter continues to live out her father's projections and expectations until she becomes *aware* of how embedded they are in her personal and professional identity. This awareness usually comes about as the result of a disillusioning experience with a father figure—most typically, a spouse, partner, or boss. In the example of the playhouse, I projected my unmet fantasies, activated by my relationship with my father, onto my husband, sabotaging every effort to actualize them on my own. A father's daughter may also transfer her yearning for recognition and approval, *and* her web of projections and expectations, from her father to her boss. Typically, she receives the approval she craves, as long as she keeps the unspoken covenant (initially made with the father and transferred to the boss) to remain loyal. If she dares to assert an independent point of view, however, the rift that results may force her to confront her buried projections. Whenever a father's daughter initiates a change in her interactions with the men in her life, she takes an important step in differentiating herself from her father.

Danielle, whom we met in chapter 2, worked successfully as the project director of a managed health-care corporation for ten years. Her boss, twelve years her senior, was a visionary in this arid field and highly respected for his innovative ideas about delivering health services to prevent serious illnesses. Danielle was his "first lieutenant," devoted to his vision and tireless in implementing his ideas. For many years, their professional relationship was stimulating and nurturing (and, for a short period of time, intimate), but when the corporation began to expand, her boss underwent dramatic changes in his personality. He became paranoid and controlling, fearing that his colleagues, including her, were trying to "mess with" his ideas. At staff meetings, he became rigid and autocratic when employees voiced ideas that differed even slightly from his. When Danielle tried to talk to him in private about his attitude toward staff members and about the validity of their proposals, he accused her of being disloyal and naive. To her shock, he then began to ignore or ridicule her suggestions in staff meetings.

Danielle began to realize that her relationship with her boss in some ways replicated her relationship with her father. As long as she had agreed with her father and had not brought up anything unpleasant, he was affable and effusive: but whenever she had tried to present her point of view, he would instantly withdraw his respect and affection. Danielle was afraid of her boss's anger and rejection, just as she had been afraid of her father's. Her boss's continued humiliation of her in front of others forced her to realize that the only way she could continue her job would be to parrot his ideas—ideas with which she no longer agreed. Her choices were to remain silent and invisible as a loyal daughter, to express herself and face intimidation and repercussions, or to leave.

Danielle finally chose to leave her job. This was a heart-wrenching decision because, in doing so, she lost the community she had helped to develop as well as her relationship with a man whom she had loved and respected. In severing her connection with this "father," Danielle felt like an outcast; for months, she was plagued by nagging doubts about her decision. Eventually, Danielle realized that leaving her job had been a crucial step toward regaining herself. In withdrawing her projections about who she wanted her boss to be, as well as ending the cycle of performance for his approval, she no longer felt split within. In the process, she found her voice, and as a consequence, she eventually began a more honest dialogue with her own father.

Finding her inner authority and voicing it to her father is often a daunting task for a father's daughter. She has been so enmeshed with her father that *any* step toward a separate identity, even disagreement, is experienced, metaphorically, like a death. Claire, whom we met in chapter 4, was so enmeshed with her father that she clung to her image of him as war hero and protector well into her fifties. Her father was away from the family for four years during World War II, and Claire yearned for his protection from the cold, biting rage of her alcoholic mother. When her father returned, he never addressed his wife's mood swings; he became absorbed in his job as the doctor in a small Southern town.

In adulthood, Claire continued to harbor an unconscious childhood yearning to be protected by her father. She kept that unmet hope alive until she became aware that the coping strategies she had developed as a child to survive the pain of his absence were influencing her current life. Her "happy face" persona had been deeply etched over time to protect her from her mother as well as to please her father, and she decided she no longer wanted to wear it through life. She made a promise to herself to stop performing for others' expectations and to stop projecting her need for protection onto others. At the same time, she had a dream that indicated an acceptance by her psyche that her father would never be her savior. She dreamed:

> There is a little girl in the desert dressed in warm, dark, coarse Bedouin clothes. Hornets swarm around her as she is cast out by the tribe and left in the desert. Her father, who is the Sheik of Araby, is gone, but he is supposed to return to find her. As the girl watches the tribespeople walk away, she hopes that her father will come, but she knows, as does everyone else, that he will never return. She is left to die as an outcast.

Claire dreams herself as a young girl in the desert, waiting for her father to return. Hornets have already begun to encircle her, knowing that she has been left to die. These insects, however, symbolize spontaneous regeneration. The daughter within Claire, who longs for her father to rescue her from her mother, must die and be reborn in order for the woman to become whole.

Although this was a frightening dream, Claire realized that it was an important step in her individuation process. When she first awoke from the dream, she felt angry at the women for colluding with the rest of the tribe to abandon the child, but she knew in her heart that the child could survive on her own. Claire has come to understand that her father's denial of her mother's alcoholism prevented him from protecting her and her siblings. Accepting him as he *is*, without the mantle of her heroic projections, Claire is now psychologically free to disidentify from him and move on alone.

At this point in her life, Claire has fulfilled her duties as wife and mother. Recently divorced after a thirty-year marriage, she has developed a successful career and is confident that she can provide for her own security. She has also come to accept that she can protect herself, and although she feels that she is taking baby steps to find out who she is, she no longer carries the suffocating fear of her childhood in her heart.

In these two examples, each woman described herself as an *outcast* in leaving the father. Danielle literally cast herself out of the community she loved when she disagreed with her boss; in Claire's dream, the tribe cast her out to wander alone in the desert. The outcast is a powerful metaphor of a woman alone on her quest,[2] and the desert is a symbol of the barren starting point of the journey each woman must make to reclaim her soul.[3] Leaving the consensual comfort of collective consciousness, the father's daughter separates herself from the father, from the old attitudes that have ruled her psyche. She lays to rest the outmoded childlike identification of herself bound to her father—the web of projections and expectations—and begins the difficult work of searching in the desert for the bones of her deeper Self.

The Internal Father

Most daughters have two fathers—their personal fathers and their internal fathers, the fathers-inside-their-heads.[4] The personal father has a life independent from his daughter; he reads the paper, goes to work, plays racquetball, gardens, sits, thinks, prays, eats, makes love, sleeps, and has his own dreams. He ages, and one day he dies. The internal father has no such human limitations. He is ever present, ever watchful, ever expectant, ever judgmental. He *always* has something to say—a litany of directives, promises, warnings, and expectations. *Don't disappoint me. Don't let me down. Make me proud. Be a good girl.* In order to receive the undivided attention of the internal father, the father's daughter must remain enmeshed in his web.

In her essay "Two for the Price of One," Sara Maitland writes:

> The Father in my head holds me in a double blackmail: if you are good I will cherish you *and* if you are bad I will punish you. . . .
> In exchange for the rewards, the punishments, and the constant attention, I am strong and never ill, and I am industrious and

look after my husband and children, and I am professional and competent and tough. I never get too angry, too sad, or too mad. I exercise control and charm and good manners and I do not run off to the woods at night when the moon is full to grunt and wallow with the sows or howl with the wolf cubs. I ignore, or spank, the little girl who wants to scream or sulk or play in the mud or eat too many ice creams.[5]

The internal father combines aspects of the personal father and the archetypal father and is therefore fraught with the weight of the archetypal promise and demand. He parades in a variety of personas and temperaments, depending upon the personal, religious, and cultural images that peopled the daughter's early years. He pervades and confuses her other relationships with spouse, friend, boss, even God.[6] His life is not of the material realm, yet he never leaves her side. At times he is silent, yet he is always *there*. She pays for the soothing aspects of his presence, protection, and attention with feelings of fear, guilt, and inadequacy because of her inability to be perfect. To identify the internal father in her psyche, a father's daughter has to uncover both the positive messages she has internalized from her personal father as well as the impossible, and often imaginary, demands and promises she is still trying to keep.

As previously discussed, a father's daughter has typically internalized affirming messages from her father about her competence, talents, and intellectual abilities. She cherishes her equality with men and her superiority to women, and she feels entitled to get what she wants. She has also internalized negative messages that bind her to the internal father she continually strives to please. If her internal father demands perfection, a father's daughter will never feel satisfied with what she achieves in her life. If he demands undying love, she may never feel free to bond intimately with a lover. If he demands her unwavering loyalty, she will steadfastly serve his ideas and values. If he demands her continued dependence, she will remain an emotional prostitute.

Eventually, the threads of projection and expectation that constitute the internal father begin to unravel as the father's daughter learns to identify his voice in her head. She learns that a particular tone or word or feeling signals his presence. She catches herself in midadmonishment: *"Don't stop now; you'll never get anywhere." "Stick with what you know." "You can't really mean that!" "He's a nice guy, but he doesn't make enough money." "Don't do it that way; that's too impractical."* But if she listens more carefully, she hears subterranean thoughts and desires that are foreign to those of the internal father. In the deeper recesses of her being, she knows how she truly wants to live her life, and she begins to make decisions that reflect what will feed her *soul*. The voice of the internal father can inform her, but it no longer *rules* her; *hers* is now the dominant voice in her head.

The father's daughter then can begin to "grow" a new kind of internal father, a voice that is softer and more connected to her feelings and respectful of her limitations. This new father encourages her to say no to self-imposed heroic requests, even as he supports her desire to actualize her dreams and inspirations. As she develops this new relationship with an accepting, nurturing, more expansive *internal* father, she develops empathy not only for herself but for her *personal* father as well. Enmeshment dissolves, and integration begins.

When the father of a father's daughter dies, her relationship with the internal father may transform as well. No longer locked in habitual behavioral patterns or power struggles with her personal father, the daughter feels freer to change her interactions with the father-inside-her-head. As she does the psychological work of healing old wounds by reconciling herself to the loss of her father as well as acknowledging the gifts she has received from him, the dialogue with her internal father may soften, allowing her to develop a more compassionate relationship to herself.

Healing Old Wounds

Throughout the process of relinquishing her idealization of her father, a father's daughter grows to accept him as a man. To fully experience his value, however, she needs to acknowledge the wounds of disappointment and loss. She may have the courage to express these directly to her father, or if this is not possible, she may find expression in art, in a therapeutic relationship, or in interactions with supportive friends, family members, or her spouse.

During the last session of my ongoing women's group on the father-daughter relationship, we create a ritual of severance, taken from the tradition of the native American "vision quest." Each woman describes the wounds from her relationship with her father (many with anger and regret) and their impact in other areas of her life. She then writes them on a piece of paper, and together as a group, we burn the papers ceremonially. We release our fathers from blame, bless them, and take responsibility for ourselves. In this way, each woman demonstrates her willingness to let go of her role as *daughter* and fully lay claim to her life with the loving support of a compassionate circle of women.

Danielle released her belief that she had been damaged by her father's inability to see her as a unique and separate person, and she acknowledged her awareness that she can do this for herself. Nancy relinquished her resentment of her father's refusal to accept her weakness, sadness, and loneliness, understanding his inability to accept those feelings in himself. She knows that she has to express these feelings, no matter how painful they may be. Kris released the fear of abandonment that has permeated her relationships with men ever since her father died when she was a child. Her father left her unprotected from an abusive mother, but she can stop the cycle of abuse by lovingly caring for herself.

It takes time, attention, and courage to heal the wounds of loss, and a ritual of severence is not a magic pill. But it does provide a spiritual container for a woman's healing process; she is no longer a victim or a child. One woman described how her understanding about the complexities of both her enmeshment with her father and her estrangement from her mother gave her an insight into the ambiguities of life. She said, "In some perverse way, I gained a jewel from the experience of being so close to the underlying tension between my dad and mom. I see how I have internalized those conflicting elements within myself, and I now realize—not just intellectually, *but in my bones*—the ambiguity of life. There's almost nothing I see or hear that I don't understand."

Once a father's daughter ceases to hold her father accountable for failing to fulfill her yearnings, she is free from her struggle to separate from him. Healing the wounds of their relationship, she can now focus fully on living her life. She doesn't have to *prove* herself anymore: she doesn't need a man to validate her decisions. She is free to love and respect her spouse or partner openly in a relationship based on mutual acceptance. She can use her skills and imagination to provide for and protect herself. She can be honest with herself about her ambition or the lack of it; she can find the energy to pursue her own dreams *when* they emerge. She can listen to her inner rhythms, making time for play as well as work. She can take her life seriously, but with humor—she already knows how to be responsible; what she has to learn now is how to let go. No longer needing to be fiercely independent, she can ask for help and accept it from both women and men, understanding the interdependence between herself and others. No person can function and make a creative contribution to the collective alone.[7] She can listen to the voice of women's wisdom and hear the sound of her own deep spirit within. She can love her father with her arms wide open, no longer needing to cling to him.

Gifts of the Father

A father's daughter fully reconciles with her father only when she can perceive his true gifts. This occurs, paradoxically, when she no longer *needs* him to validate her authority, and when she is separate enough to honor her own wisdom. She can then discern what her father truly *gave* her instead of what she *wanted* him to give. In *The Gift*, Lewis Hyde writes that a gift must always be used, consumed, and eaten. "The gift that is not used will be lost, while the one that is passed along remains abundant."[8] The true gifts of the father are often hidden from his daughter until she is ready to reclaim them.

Noriko is a Japanese-Canadian pharmacist in her forties. Her father recently died, and she returned to Japan for the first time in twenty years to honor his death. She wanted a remembrance from her father's daily life; something he touched, used, and clearly valued. She was pleased to receive his large wooden abacus. Her father had owned a rice-flour mill in Japan and used the abacus, as his father had before him, to keep the books for the mill. With it he also managed the finances of the local political party.

Noriko grew up in a small hamlet in post–World War II Japan. She worked for her father in the mill, delivering orders and invoices on her bike. Over time, she became adept at using the abacus; as her young fingers flew across the beads, she absorbed the daily workings of the business. When she became a pharmacist years later, her skill at counting beads came in handy, enhancing her speed at sorting medications. Now she runs her own pharmacy.

Noriko's father had prevented his children from having any kind of relationship with their mother, because she had contracted tuberculosis after the war and was forced to live apart as an outcast. Since Noriko was the firstborn daughter in a family with no son, it was the cultural expectation that she would take over her father's business. When Noriko wanted to emigrate to Canada in her early twenties, she expected her father to forbid her. Instead, he said nothing in response to her announcement. She was confused when he refused to discuss it and then devastated when he did nothing to dissuade her.

At that time, it was highly unusual for a single Japanese woman to leave her family, let alone the country, with little knowledge of other languages and with no guarantee of a job. The expectation was that the oldest would stay, marry, and care for the family. Noriko left with neither her father's support nor his blessing. She gave up her inheritance, divesting herself of all family ties. Her father's silence broke her heart; only later did she realize that in keeping his silence he was also giving her her freedom. While Noriko's father could not give his blessing within the constraints of their culture, neither did he forbid her to leave, which was ultimately the greatest gift he could give her. A true gift of love always involves personal sacrifice.

One of the gifts nineteen-year-old Lydia received from her father was an enduring sense of security, which was symbolized for her by one poignant experience. The night before she entered junior high, she was very upset and nervous. She had a premonition that her experience in seventh grade would be difficult. Her father listened to her fears and then left their apartment and drove to the schoolyard. Symbols and rituals held great value for him, so he searched the yard for a simple rock to bring back to his daughter. Lydia said, "The rock was a 'magic pill' for me; it helped me ease into school. I took it with me when I transferred to another school the following year. It wasn't really the rock that made me feel better; it was my father's gesture. I was very young and very scared, and he made me feel secure."

A father may never know how much he has given his daughter, and a daughter may not immediately understand the meaning of his gift. It becomes clear as time passes, however, and perhaps long after his death. His time, presence, values, and the tools of his trade are often taken for granted. But they provide clues to the mystery of the man who is father. Like Noriko's abacus and Lydia's rock, they signify love.

Last summer, Danielle invited her parents to travel with her to

France. They had scrimped to send her abroad for her junior year in college and now, thirty years later, she wanted to return the gift. At eighty-six and in failing health, her father had never expected to have the opportunity to return to Europe. Danielle discovered that the true gift of the trip emerged in watching her father's awe at the dawn of each new day. She said, "He was so filled with joy—just like a child. He saw life as a gift, which, in turn, he gave to me as I watched the wonder in his eyes. We had a real coming together. I know that it will help me when he dies to have had this time with him. I now have something to draw upon, both spiritually and emotionally." Being able to share this joy with her father gave Danielle a profound sense of her own adequacy and of her deep gratitude to her father.

———

As I compose my final thoughts for this book, I fear that I have looked both too closely at my relationship with my own father and not closely enough. I am my father's daughter, both devotee and traitor. I come from him. I am of him, and I can never know the whole of him. I only know what he has revealed to me through his love, actions, and omissions. The rest remains a mystery.

I have my father's easy smile, wide hands, high cheekbones. I look at the world visually, assessing it with his aesthetic. My love of rhododendrons, the sea, and reading mystery books is his. I share his compulsive need to be active, inability to sleep, and love of nature. I carry forth his desire to understand all points of view, as well as an Irish opinionatedness that often negates it. His curiosity, creativity, and deep satisfaction with his work inspire me; his need to control rankles me and reminds me of my own. I love my children with his ferocity and possessiveness. The father of my youth was kind and loving, yet impossible to please. How I have longed for his protection and approval. At last, I have released this yearning. I have been deeply blessed by his spirit and presence, wounded by his absence, and resolved to them both. Only now can I begin to fully accept his love.

I started this book with a dream, a dream about my father's death. I was afraid of the dream, afraid that it was a portent of what would happen if I continued to explore our relationship. Yet I also knew that the death of the father, like that of the king, signals the death of the old ruling attitudes of the psyche. This death would be absolutely necessary if I was to learn who *I* am. What have I learned about being a father's daughter? I started this journey of discovery from the vantage point of being a *daughter*, fearful of hurting my father's feelings, yearning for his attention and approval, holding him responsible for not protecting me or building my dreams. I have untangled the knotted threads of the archetypal promise made between the two of us, and I know that it is not his—or anyone else's—responsibility to provide for or protect me now. I have to do that myself. I have not killed my father in writing this book; I have killed my struggle to *become him*.

Maureen Murdock and her father.
Photo by Lucien Wulsin, Jr.

EPILOGUE

To the Fathers of the Future

> If fathers allow personal and cultural patterns of the status quo to lull them to sleep, then they may lose their children in the process. If fathers truly want deep connection with their children and are willing to do the work, I believe it will come to them, although its form may surprise them.
>
> —Charles Scull, *Fathers*

MANY of the women in this book who have shared their stories with you, asked me if I thought fathers would read this book. I certainly hope so. The role of father has evolved over time, and with each new epoch, his role has expanded to include the functions of fathers of previous generations. The needs of daughters have evolved over time as well. My daughter's generation, and the daughters her generation will bring into this world, will be challenged in ways that you and I have merely dreamed possible. These daughters will need their father's support to become full women who are honored and respected for themselves as females, not for their ability to emulate men and reflect their father's identity.

Emily, a father's daughter in her forties who has had a series of difficult relationships with men throughout her adulthood, ended our interview with a poignant plea to the fathers she hoped would read this book. "Please tell them to love their wives. It would have been so much easier for me if my father had loved me less, and loved my mother more." To honor Emily's request, I have a few suggestions for the fathers of tomorrow:

Be affectionate and love your wife; model the joys of a full and loving relationship.

Read to your daughter, sing to her, listen to her fantasies. Encourage her in her abilities to make her dreams come true.

Teach her specific skills, coach her in team sports, show her how to use tools. But don't force her to become a tomboy to get your attention. Let her be a little girl, and honor her femininity.

Allow your daughter to express the full range of her emotions. Listen, but don't try to fix her feelings. Trust that if she knows you accept her, she will be able to find her own solutions.

Laugh with her, cry with her, feel your own emotions. Don't expect her to take care of your feelings, and never depend upon her to be your emotional wife.

Respect her privacy; her body is hers. As she enters adolescence, find appropriate support to deal with your discomfort about her emerging sexuality.

Trust her to choose her own lovers, and bless her choice of a spouse.

Let her know that there is more to life than meets the eye; respect her intuition and honor her sense of spirit.

Affirm her desire to make a positive contribution to the world.

Know when it is time to let go, and befriend her as you both grow in wisdom.

Be gentle with her as you go into the night.

NOTES

Chapter One

1. Definition of a "good enough" father from Dr. Marlin S. Potash, quoted in Victoria Secunda, *Women and Their Fathers* (New York: Delacorte Press, 1992), 101.

2. Adrienne Rich, *Of Woman Born: Motherhood as Experience and Institution* (New York: W. W. Norton, 1976), 249.

3. Mary Gordon, "The Parable of the Cave or: In Praise of Watercolors," in *The Writer on Her Work*, ed. Janet Sternburg (New York: Norton, 1980), 31–32.

Chapter Two

1. T. Berry Brazelton: presentation at the 12th Annual Margaret S. Mahler Symposium, Philadelphia (1981), cited in Signe Hammer, *Passionate Attachments* (New York: Rawson Associates, 1982), 131.

2. Betty Carter, "Fathers and Daughters," in *The Invisible Web: Gender Patterns in Family Relationships*, ed. Marianne Walters (New York: Guilford Press, 1988), 99.

3. Elizabeth Mehren, "Cues from the Crib," *Los Angeles Times*, 20 May 1992, E1, E8.

4. Robert Johnson, *Owning Your Own Shadow* (San Francisco: Harper & Row, 1991), 26.

5. Carter, "Fathers and Daughters," 102.

Chapter Three

1. Hammer, *Passionate Attachments*, (New York; Rawson Associates, 1982), 137–8.

2. Bruno Bettelheim, *The Uses of Enchantment: The Meaning and Importance of Fairy Tales* (New York: Vintage Books, 1977), 307.

3. Andrew Samuels, "On Fathering Daughters," *Psychological Perspectives* 21 (Fall 1989): 129.

4. Irene Gad, "The Couple in Fairy Tales: When Father's Daughter Meets Mother's Son," in *Psyche's Stories*, ed. Murray Stein and Lionel Corbett (Wilmette, Ill.: Chiron Publications, 1991), 40–41.

5. Julia Jewett, " 'Allerleirauh' (All Kinds of Fur): A Tale of Father Dominance, Psychological Incest, and Female Emergence" in Stein and Corbett, *Psyche's Stories*, 24.

6. Linda Schierse Leonard, *The Wounded Woman* (Boston: Shambhala Publications, 1982), 159. Leonard writes that a father can function as a "ghostly lover" when there is a "too positive" relation with the father or when the father is absent. She states: "Often an idealized relation to the father is built up unconsciously when the father is missing."

7. Samuels, "On Fathering Daughters," 126–9.

8. Barbara Smith, "The Roy and Barbara Show," performed at Highways in Santa Monica, Calif., 6 June 1991.

9. Jewett, " 'Allerleirauh,' " 17–18.

10. Carter, "Fathers and Daughters," 99.

11. Lynda E. Boose, "The Father's House and the Daughter in It," in *Daughters and Fathers*, ed. Lynda E. Boose and Betty S. Flowers (Baltimore: Johns Hopkins University Press, 1989), 68.

12. Ibid., 69.

13. Ibid.

14. Connie Zweig, "Failing My Father, Finding Myself," in *Fathers, Sons and Daughters*, ed. Charles Scull (Los Angeles: Jeremy P. Tarcher, 1992), 132.

15. Ibid., 134.

16. Ibid.

17. See Ellen Bass and Laura Davis, *The Courage to Heal* (New York: Harper & Row, 1988); Sandra Butler, *Conspiracy of Silence: The Trauma of Incest* (San Francisco: Volcano Press, 1985); Judith Herman, *Father-Daughter Incest* (Cambridge: Harvard University Press, 1981); Alice Miller, *Thou Shalt Not Be Aware: Society's Betrayal of the Child* (New York:

New American Library, 1986); Michelle Morris, *If I Should Die Before I Wake* (New York: Dell, 1982); Florence Rush, *The Best Kept Secret: Sexual Abuse of Children* (Englewood Cliffs: Prentice-Hall, 1980); Jeffrey Masson, *The Assault on Truth: Freud's Suppression of the Seduction Theory* (New York: Farrar, Straus & Giroux, 1984).

18. Jane Carruth, *The Giant All-Color Book of Fairy Tales* (New York: Golden Press, 1971), 334–349.

19. Jewett, " 'Allerleirauh,' " 24.

Chapter Four

1. Marion Woodman, *Leaving My Father's House* (Boston: Shambhala Publications, 1992), 13.

2. Daryl Sharp, *Jung Lexicon* (Toronto: Inner City Books, 1991), 29.

3. Carl Jung, *Freud and Psychoanalysis* (New York: Bollingen Series XX, 1961), 323.

4. Carl Jung, *Psyche and Symbol* (New York: Doubleday, 1958), 135–136.

5. For a full discussion of the journey of the hero, see Joseph Campbell, *A Hero with a Thousand Faces* (Princeton: Bollingen Series XVII, 1949).

6. June Singer, "Finding the Lost Feminine in the Judeo-Christian Tradition," in *To Be a Woman*, ed. Connie Zweig (Los Angeles: Jeremy P. Tarcher, 1990), 224–225.

7. The female counterpart to the hero's journey is the heroine's journey, which defines the quest of modern-day woman to reclaim and heal her feminine nature. See Maureen Murdock, *The Heroine's Journey* (Boston: Shambhala Publications, 1990).

8. Dr. Augustus Napier, address to American Association of Marriage and Family Therapists conference, San Francisco, October, 1990.

9. Sharon Olds, "Looking at My Father," in *The Gold Cell* (New York: Alfred A. Knopf, 1990), 31.

10. Ibid., 31–32.

11. Mary Gordon, *The Other Side* (New York: Penguin Books, 1989), 357.

12. I first read about fathers "missing in action" in Brenda Peterson's essay, "The War That Fell to Earth" in *Nature and Other Mothers* (New York: HarperCollins, 1992), 171–175.

13. Hammer, *Passionate Attachments*, 207.

14. Shirley Abbott, *The Bookmaker's Daughter* (New York: Ticknor & Fields, 1991), 185.

15. Ibid., 181.

16. Ibid., 264.

17. Gilda Frantz, "Birth's Cruel Secret/O I am my own Lost Mother/To my own Sad Child," in *Chiron: A Review of Jungian Analysis,* (Chiron Publications, 1985): 157–158.

18. Marion Woodman, *The Ravaged Bridegroom* (Toronto: Inner City Books, 1990), 115.

19. Ibid., 112.

Chapter Five

1. Arthur Colman and Libby Colman, *Earth Father, Sky Father* (Englewood Cliffs, N.J.: Prentice-Hall, 1981), 78.

2. Gordon, "Parable of the Cave," 31.

3. Ibid., 32.

4. Albert Kreinheder, "The Jealous Father Syndrome," *Psychological Perspectives* 2, no. 1 (Spring 1971): 45–46.

5. Ibid.

6. Colman and Colman, *Earth Father, Sky Father*, 14.

7. The Brothers Grimm, *The Complete Grimm's Fairy Tales* (New York: Pantheon Books, 1944), 160–166.

8. Ibid., 160.

9. Ibid., 161.

10. Ibid.

11. Ibid.

12. Ibid.

Chapter Six

1. Robert Moore and Douglas Gillette, *King, Warrior, Magician, Lover* (San Francisco: HarperCollins, 1990). See 49–73 for a detailed discussion of the King archetype.

2. Karen E. Klein, "Low-Income Housing Was Dad's Dream," *Los Angeles Times*, 22 March 1992, K1.

3. Starhawk, *Truth or Dare* (San Francisco: Harper & Row, 1987), 66.

4. Quoted in Lynn Smith, "Protesting Patriarch," *Los Angeles Times*, 16 May 1993, E1.

5. Starhawk, *Truth or Dare*, 66.

6. Hammer, *Passionate Attachments*, 217.

7. For a full discussion of women's psychological growth and moral development, see Carol Gilligan, *In a Different Voice: Psychological Theory and Women's Development*. Cambridge: Harvard University Press, 1982.

8. Jean Baker Miller, "Women and Power," *Journal: Women and Therapy 6*, nos. 1 and 2 (Spring/Summer 1987): 1–11.

9. Jean Block's research is discussed in Nicky Marone, *How to Father a Successful Daughter* (New York: McGraw-Hill, 1988), 92. For more information, see Jean H. Block, "Another Look at Sex Differentiation in the Socialization Behaviors of Mothers and Fathers," in J. A. Sherman and F. L. Denmark (eds.), *Psychology of Women: Future Directions of Research* (New York: Psychological Dimensions, 1979).

10. Ibid. For more information on "learned helplessness," see *Journal of Abnormal Psychology*, 87 (1) (February 1978), which dealt solely with this issue.

11. Barbara Marsh, "Daughters Find That Fathers Still Resist Passing the Family Business on to Them," *The Wall Street Journal*, 14 April 1992, B1.

12. Ibid.

13. Ibid., B2.

14. For a full discussion of the managerial woman, see Margaret Hennig and Anne Jardim, *The Managerial Woman* (Garden City, N.Y.: Anchor Press/Doubleday, 1977).

15. Discussed in Hammer, *Passionate Attachments*, 201.

16. Cantor and Bernay, *Women in Power*, 103–109.

17. Quoted in Connie Zweig and Jeremiah Abrams, *Meeting the Shadow* (Los Angeles: Jeremy P. Tarcher, 1991), 48.

18. Ibid., 49.

19. W. G. Clark and W. Aldis Wright, eds., *The Complete Works of William Shakespeare* (Programmed Classics), 759.

20. Ibid.

21. Ibid., 760.

22. Ibid.

23. Ibid.

24. Ibid., 761.

25. James Kirsch, *Shakespeare's Royal Self* (New York: C. G. Jung Foundation for Analytical Psychology, 1966), 194.

26. Clark and Wright, *Complete Works of Shakespeare*, 791.

27. Starhawk, *Truth or Dare*, 10.

28. Ibid., 21.

29. Ibid., 10.

30. Cantor and Bernay, *Women in Power*, 28.

Chapter Seven

1. Moore and Gillette, *King, Warrior, Magician, Lover*, 49.
2. Ibid., 56.
3. Sherry Ruth Anderson and Patricia Hopkins, eds., *The Feminine Face of God* (New York: Bantam Books, 1991), 28.
4. Ibid., 28–29.
5. Carol P. Christ, *Laughter of Aphrodite* (San Francisco: Harper & Row, 1987), 97–98.
6. Ibid., 98–99.
7. Charlene Spretnak, ed., *The Politics of Women's Spirituality* (New York: Anchor Press, 1982), xii.
8. See Marija Gimbutas, *Goddesses and Gods of Old Europe, 7000–3500 B.C.* (Berkeley and Los Angeles: University of California Press, 1982).
9. Barbara Walker, *The Skeptical Feminist* (San Francisco: Harper & Row, 1987), 133.
10. See Gimbutas, *Goddesses and Gods*; and Merlin Stone, *When God Was a Woman* (San Diego: Harcourt Brace Jovanovich, 1978).
11. Spretnak, *Politics of Women's Spirituality*, 394.
12. Barbara Walker, *The Crone* (San Francisco: Harper & Row, 1985), 19.
13. Barbara Walker, *The Woman's Dictionary of Symbols and Sacred Objects* (San Francisco: Harper & Row, 1988), 275.
14. Anderson and Hopkins, *Feminine Face of God*, 77.
15. Alice Walker, *The Color Purple* (London: Women's Press, 1983), 66–67.

Chapter Eight

1. Sharon Olds, "Last Words," in *The Father* (New York: Alfred A. Knopf, 1992), 23.
2. Carolyn G. Heilbrun, *Writing a Woman's Life* (New York: Ballantine Books, 1988), 64–65.
3. Victoria Secunda, *Women and Their Fathers* (New York: Delacorte Press, 1992), 365.
4. Diane Elizabeth Dreher, *Domination and Defiance: Fathers and Daughters in Shakespeare* (Lexington, Ky.: University Press of Kentucky, 1986), 166.

5. Ibid., 43–44.

6. Ibid., 44.

7. Abbott, *Bookmaker's Daughter*, 264–265.

8. Ibid., 265.

9. Ibid., 267.

10. Collette Dowling, *The Cinderella Complex* (New York: Summit Books, 1981), 18.

11. Gloria Steinem, *Revolution from Within* (Boston: Little, Brown & Co., 1992), 264.

12. Ibid., 264–265.

13. This old Jewish story was first told to me by Gilda Frantz in 1991. The issues this story illuminates about betrayal and trust are analyzed in depth in James Hillman, "Betrayal," *Spring: An Annual of Jungian Thought and Archetypal Psychology* (Analytic Psychology Club of New York, Inc., 1965): 57–76.

14. Hillman, *"Betrayal,"* 60.

15. Ibid., 61.

16. Ibid., 72.

17. Ibid., 76.

18. Madonna Kolbenschlag, *Kiss Sleeping Beauty Good-bye* (San Francisco: Harper & Row, 1979), 169.

19. Iona and Peter Opic, *The Classic Fairy Tales*. (London: Oxford University Press, 1974), 139–150.

20. Larry Gates, "The Resurrection of the Body in Cocteau's *Beauty and the Beast*," *Psychological Perspectives* 23 (Spring 1991): 112–123.

21. Ibid., 123.

Chapter Nine

1. Clarissa Pinkola Estes, *Women Who Run with the Wolves* (New York: Ballantine Books, 1992), 395.

2. Ibid., 412.

3. See Maureen Murdock, *The Heroine's Journey*, chap. 5 for a discussion about spiritual aridity and death and chap. 6 for a discussion about the Descent.

4. This section on the Internal Father was inspired by Sara Maitland, "Two for the Price of One," in *Fathers: Reflections by Daughters*, ed. Ursula Owen (New York: Pantheon Books, 1983), 18–28.

5. Ibid., 26.

6. Ibid., 19.

7. Ellen Meredith, *Listening In: Dialogues with the Wiser Self* (Haydenville, Mass.: Horse Mountain Press, 1993), 166.

8. Lewis Hyde, *The Gift* (New York: Vantage Books, 1979), 21.

BIBLIOGRAPHY

Abbott, Shirley. *The Bookmaker's Daughter*. New York: Ticknor & Fields, 1991.

Anderson, Sherry Ruth, and Patricia Hopkins. *The Feminine Face of God*. New York: Bantam Books, 1991.

Bettelheim, Bruno. *The Uses of Enchantment: The Meaning and Importance of Fairy Tales*. New York: Vintage Books, 1977.

Bennett, Paula. *My Life a Loaded Gun*. Boston: Beacon Press, 1986.

Boose, Lynda E., and Betty S. Flowers. *Daughters and Fathers*. Baltimore: Johns Hopkins University Press, 1989.

Bowlby, John. *Separation, Anxiety and Anger*. New York: Basic Books, 1973.

Cantor, Dorothy W., and Toni Bernay, with Jean Stoess. *Women in Power*. New York: Houghton Mifflin Co., 1992.

Carruth, Jane. *Fairy Tales*. New York: Golden Press, 1972.

Chase, Joan. *The Evening Wolves*. New York: Farrar, Straus & Giroux, 1989.

Christ, Carol. *Laughter of Aphrodite*. San Francisco: Harper & Row, 1987.

Clark, W. G., and W. Aldis Wright, eds. *The Complete Works of William Shakespeare*.

Colman Arthur, and Libby Colman. *Earth Father, Sky Father*. Englewood Cliffs, N.J.: Prentice-Hall, 1981.

Dowling, Collette. *The Cinderella Complex*. New York: Summit Books, 1981.

Dreher, Diane Elizabeth. *Domination and Defiance: Fathers and Daughters in Shakespeare*. Lexington, Ky.: University Press of Kentucky, 1986.

Eisler, Riane. *The Chalice and the Blade*. San Francisco: Harper & Row, 1987.

Erdoes, Richard, and Alfonso Ortiz, eds. *American Indian Myths and Legends*. New York: Pantheon Books, 1984.

Estes, Clarissa Pinkola. *Women Who Run with the Wolves*. New York: Ballantine Books, 1992.

Faludi, Susan. *Backlash: The Undeclared War against American Women*. New York: Crown Publishers, 1991.

Gimbutas, Marija, *Goddesses and Gods of Old Europe, 7000–3500 B.C.* Berkeley and Los Angeles: University of California Press, 1982.

Gordon, Mary. *The Other Side*. New York: Penguin Books, 1989.

Greer, Germaine. *Daddy We Hardly Knew You*. New York: Fawcett Columbine, 1989.

Grimm, The Brothers. *The Complete Grimm's Fairy Tales*. New York: Pantheon Books, 1944.

Hammer, Signe. *Passionate Attachments*. New York: Rawson Associates, 1982.

Harding, M. Esther. *The Way of All Women*. London: Longmans, Green and Co., 1933.

Heilbrun, Carolyn G. *Writing a Woman's Life*. New York: Ballantine Books, 1988.

Hennig, Margaret, and Anne Jardim. *The Managerial Woman*. Garden City, N.Y.: Anchor Press/Doubleday, 1977.

Houston, Jean. *The Hero and the Goddess*. New York: Ballantine Books, 1992.

Hurcombe, Linda, ed. *Sex and God: Some Varieties of Women's Religious Experience*. New York and London: Routledge & Kegan Paul, 1987.

Hyde, Lewis. *The Gift*. New York: Vintage Books, 1979.

Johnson, Robert A. *Femininity Lost and Regained*. New York: Harper Perennial, 1990.

———. *Owning Your Own Shadow*. San Francisco: Harper & Row, 1991.

Jung, Carl G. *Freud and Psychoanalysis*. New York: Bollingen Series XX, 1961.

Kinsley, David. *The Goddesses' Mirror: Visions of the Divine from East and West*. Albany: State University of New York Press, 1989.

Kirsch, James. *Shakespeare's Royal Self*. New York: C. G. Jung Foundation for Analytical Psychology, 1966.

Kolbenschlag, Madonna. *Kiss Sleeping Beauty Good-Bye*. San Francisco: Harper & Row, 1979.

Kufrin, Joan. *Uncommon Women*. Piscataway, N.J.: New Century Publishers, 1981.

Kuo, Louise, and Yuan-Hsi. *Chinese Folktales*. Millbrae, Calif.: Celestial Arts, 1976.

Lamb, Michael E., ed. *The Father's Role: Cross-Cultural Perspectives.* Hillsdale, N.J.: Laurence Erlbaum Associates, Publishers, 1987.

Leonard, Linda Schierse. *The Wounded Woman.* Boston: Shambhala Publications, 1982.

Lerner, Harriet Goldhor. *Women in Therapy.* New York: Harper & Row, 1988.

Lewis, C. S. *Till We Have Faces.* New York: Harcourt, Brace & Co., 1956.

Luke, Helen M. *Woman, Earth and Spirit.* New York: Crossroad, 1984.

Marone, Nicky. *How to Father a Successful Daughter.* New York: McGraw-Hill, 1988.

Meredith, Ellen. *Listening In.* Haydenville, Mass.: Horse Mountain Press, 1993.

Miller, Jean Baker. *Toward a New Psychology of Women.* 2d ed. Boston: Beacon Press, 1986.

Miller, Sue. *Family Pictures.* New York: Harper & Row, 1990.

Minninger, Joan, and Barbara Goulter. *The Father-Daughter Dance.* New York: G. P. Putnam's Sons, 1993.

Moon, Beverly, ed. *An Encyclopedia of Archetypal Symbolism.* Boston: Shambhala Publications, 1991.

Murdock, Maureen. *The Heroine's Journey.* Boston: Shambhala Publications, 1990.

Nowra, Lousi. *Palu.* New York: St. Martin's Press, 1987.

Olds, Sharon. *The Father.* New York: Alfred A. Knopf, 1992.

———. *The Gold Cell.* New York: Alfred A. Knopf, 1990.

Owen, Ursula, ed. *Fathers: Reflections by Daughters.* New York: Pantheon Books, 1983.

Peterson, Brenda. *Nature and Other Mothers.* New York: HarperCollins, 1992.

Rich, Adrienne. *Diving into the Wreck: Poems 1971–1972.* New York: W. W. Norton, 1973.

———. *The Dream of a Common Language: Poems 1974–1977.* New York: W. W. Norton, 1978.

———. *Of Woman Born: Motherhood as Experience and Institution.* New York: W. W. Norton, 1976.

———. *Sources.* Woodside, Calif.: Heyeck Press, 1983.

Samuels, Andrew, ed. *The Father: Contemporary Jungian Perspectives.* London: Free Association Books, 1985.

Scull, Charles, ed. *Fathers, Sons and Daughters.* Los Angeles: Jeremy P. Tarcher, 1992.

Secunda, Victoria. *Women and Their Fathers.* New York: Delacorte Press, 1992.

Smiley, Jane. *A Thousand Acres*. New York: Fawcett Columbine, 1991.

Spretnak, Charlene, ed. *The Politics of Women's Spirituality*. New York: Anchor Press, 1982.

Starhawk. *Truth or Dare*. San Francisco: Harper & Row, 1987.

Stein, Murray, and Lionel Corbett. *Psyche's Stories: Modern Jungian Interpretations of Fairy Tales*. Wilmette, Ill.: Chiron Publications.

Steinem, Gloria. *Revolution from Within*. Boston: Little Brown & Co., 1992.

Sternburg, Janet, ed. *The Writer on Her Work*. New York: W. W. Norton, 1980.

Stone, Merlin. *When God Was a Woman*. San Diego: Harcourt Brace Jovanovich, 1978.

Storr, Anthony. *Churchill's Black Dog, Kafka's Mice and Other Phenomena of the Human Mind*. New York: Grove Press, 1988.

Thompson, Smith. *One Hundred Favorite Folktales*. Bloomington, Ind.: Indiana University Press, 1968.

Von Frans, Marie-Louise. *Problems of the Feminine in Fairytales*. Irving, Tex.: Spring Publications, 1972.

Walker, Alice. *The Color Purple*. London: Women's Press, 1983.

Walker, Barbara G. *The Crone*. San Francisco: Harper & Row, 1985.

———. *The Skeptical Feminist*. San Francisco: Harper & Row, 1987.

———. *The Woman's Dictionary of Symbols and Sacred Objects*. San Francisco: Harper & Row, 1988.

———. *The Woman's Encyclopedia of Myths and Secrets*. San Francisco: Harper & Row, 1983.

Walters, Marianne, Betty Carter, Peggy Papp, and Olga Silverstein, eds. *The Invisible Web: Gender Patterns in Family Relationships*. New York: Guilford Press, 1988.

Waters, Frank. *Masked Gods*. Athens: Swallow Press, 1950.

Wilmer, Harry A., ed. *Mother Father*. Wilmette, Ill.: Chiron Publications, 1990.

Wolkstein, Diane, and Samuel Noah Kramer. *Inanna, Queen of Heaven and Earth*. New York: Harper & Row, 1983.

Woodman, Marion. *Leaving My Father's House*. Boston: Shambhala Publications, 1992.

———. *The Ravaged Bridegroom*. Toronto: Inner City Books, 1990.

Young-Eisendrath, Polly and Florence L. Wiedermann. *Female Authority*. New York: Guilford Press, 1987.

Zipes, Jack. *Don't Bet on the Prince: Contemporary Feminist Fairy Tales in North America and England*. New York: Methuen, 1986.

Zweig, Connie, ed. *To Be a Woman.* Los Angeles: Jeremy P. Tarcher, 1990.

Zweig, Connie, and Jeremiah Abrams. *Meeting the Shadow.* Los Angeles: Jeremy P. Tarcher, 1991.

Articles

Frantz, Gilda. "Birth's Cruel Secret/O I am my own Lost Mother/To my own Sad Child." *Chiron: A Review of Jungian Analysis.* Chiron Publications, Wilmette, Ill. 1985, 157–172.

Koenenn, Connie. "Bent on Clearing the Air." *Los Angeles Times* (20 November, 1991): "View" section, 1–5.

Kreinheder, Albert. "The Jealous Father Syndrome." *Psychological Perspectives* 2, no. 1 (Spring 1971): 43–50.

Salzmann, Monique. "Refusing to Be a Woman." *Personal and Archetypal Dynamics in Analytical Relationships* from the Proceedings of the 11th International Congress for Analytic Psychology, Paris 89. ed. Mary Ann Mattoon. Switzerland: Daimon Verlag, 1989, 277–281.

Samuels, Andrew. "On Fathering Daughters." *Psychological Perspectives* 21 (Fall 1989): 126–9.

Schmidt, Lynda W. "How the Father's Daughter Found Her Mother." *Psychological Perspectives* 14, no. 1 (Spring 1983): 8–19.

Sellery, J'nan. "Creative Women: A Break with Tradition." *Psychological Perspectives* 11, no. 2 (Fall 1980): 109–110.

Singer, June. "Finding the Lost Feminine in the Judeo-Christian Tradition," in *To Be A Woman*, ed. Connie Zweig (Los Angeles: Jeremy P. Tarcher, 1990): 222–223.

Woodman, Marion. "Abandonment in the Creative Woman." *Chiron: A Review of Jungian Analysis.* Chiron Publications, Wilmette, Ill. 1985: 23–46.

INDEX

Kelvin Jones

About the Author

MAUREEN MURDOCK is a licensed marriage and family therapist with master's degrees in both Human Development and Family Therapy. She has twenty years' experience as an educator, lecturer, and psychotherapist and is the author of *The Heroine's Journey: Woman's Quest for Wholeness* and *Spinning Inward: Using Guided Imagery with Children*. Murdock is an artist and she teaches in the UCLA Extension Writers' Program.